# LADY
## AND THE
## TEN-TIME WORLD CHAMP

Going the Distance with Hector Macho Camacho

SHELLY SALEMASSI

Copyright © 2021 Shelly Salemassi
All rights reserved
First Edition

PAGE PUBLISHING, INC.
Conneaut Lake, PA

First originally published by Page Publishing 2021

ISBN 978-1-6624-3415-0 (pbk)
ISBN 978-1-6624-3416-7 (digital)

Printed in the United States of America

To my best friend in the world, Robert Agar, who encouraged and supported me to finish this project.

# PROLOGUE

I'm sitting on a Boeing 727 on the tarmac in Detroit.

Delta flight 582, nonstop to LaGuardia.

I've taken this hop to New York many times before—I could do it in my sleep—but this time, it will be very different. That's for certain. I'm not sure what to expect from this trip though. I have no idea what's going to happen when I get to the Bronx, let alone what I'm going to do with the rest of my life. The only thing I know for sure is this: he won't be picking me up from the airport…because he's dead.

My god, he's really gone. I still can't grasp it. Hector Camacho, one of the greatest boxers of his age and the one great love of my life, is dead at the age of fifty. If this were a nightmare, he'd have awoken me from it by now. That's the only way I know this is real.

A flight attendant has closed the boarding door and tells us to turn off our cell phones, and a crew member standing in the airport Jetway has disconnected the plane from the gate. But we're not moving; we're not going anywhere yet. The pilot just came on the radio to tell us he's waiting for clearance to taxi to the runway for our departure.

"Thank you for your patience," he says. Patience. For some reason, that made me laugh.

Sitting on this grounded airplane is the perfect metaphor for how I've felt over the last few days: in limbo. Suspended, numb, between heaven and earth. Still in this life, but not really alive.

Everything is up in the air, except me. I'm stuck in Detroit. Like I said, an apt metaphor.

How did I get on this roller coaster? And why did it suddenly plunge to the earth? I've spent over fifteen years trying to work things out with Macho. I've never worked on anything as diligently as I worked on my relationship with Macho. I've never fought harder. And I've never wanted to go the distance with anyone before. Not until I met Macho. Everything was different with him. And *he* was different. We were two of a kind, two fighters. And now he's gone. I'm standing in the ring alone.

\* \* \* \* \*

Nine days ago, Tuesday, November 20, I was playing pool at a bar when my cell phone rang. It was my sister, so I picked up. She was in a frantic state, and the bar was crowded with loud drinkers and music, so I had a hard time understanding her. I heard her say "Macho" and "Turn on the news" and "Someone shot them" and "I'm so sorry."

I thought I also heard the word *dead*, so I ran outside, holding off my hysteria, until I could ask her to clarify. On the street, things got only slightly better: she told me Macho was still alive but in critical condition. So I ran back into the bar and asked the bartender to turn on the news.

Macho and his childhood friend Adrian Moreno had been shot in Puerto Rico, near where they had grown up. It was a drive-by shooting, and there were no suspects so far. Adrian had died instantly, but Macho was holding on. That didn't surprise me at all. Macho didn't just fight in the ring; in a way, every single day of his life was a battle. I knew he wouldn't give up easily. In fact, one of the doctors who was interviewed on television had said he expected Macho to pull through, though he also hypothesized that Macho might be partially paralyzed from the bullet, which had pierced his jaw and fractured two of the vertebrae in his neck.

I knew better than that doctor did, of course. I'd watched Macho punish himself with cocaine for most of the fifteen years we'd been together. I knew he wasn't up for this fight. So when I heard one reporter warn of the danger of "cardiac arrest," I knew Macho wouldn't survive this fight. I knew he was down for the count. And so was I. For the first time, we were *both* about to get knocked out.

That was when the fog started slowly rolling in, in that shitty little bar. Time started running in fits and starts, like an old jalopy on its last leg. I drifted in and out of awareness. Without knowing how I'd gotten there, I realized I was kneeling on the floor, next to a pool table, sobbing. Someone (a friend, maybe?) was holding me. My face was hot and wet. My phone was ringing.

The next time I emerged from the fog, I was home, sitting at my computer, clicking between news and travel websites. It was after midnight, technically Wednesday morning, the day before Thanksgiving, which meant it was impossible to find a reasonably priced flight from Detroit to San Juan. I sat there, numb, trying to navigate through this obstacle course, but the fog was relentless. And the grief was exhausting. I drifted in and out of sleep…

Macho came to say goodbye to me while my head lay on that keyboard. It felt so real. Well, *surreal*. Super real. I wasn't dreaming, and I wasn't awake. This was better than either of those two planes. I could feel him holding me. I was safer than I had ever felt. In our fifteen years together, whenever we had held onto each other, I'd always felt like everything would be all right. And this time was no different, except this time, *he* had come to *me*. In life, it had always been the other way around.

"Remember that plane in Orlando, mama?" he whispered.

We both laughed, a little sadly, at that memory: I had traveled a lot during our relationship, always flying to meet him, wherever he was, at the drop of a hat. "I need you here, mama," he'd say, and I'd be on the next plane. To Orlando, to New York, wherever he asked me to go and for whatever reason. Sometimes he'd be waiting at the airport with flowers or a piece of jewelry he'd picked out for me. We would always rejoice at the sight of each other. That first embrace, at all those airport reconnections, was always filled with bottomless passion, joy, comfort, even relief. Once, he got my arrival time wrong, so he wasn't at the airport when I landed. I was furious, and I told him, "Next time, I'll turn right around and fly back home." He just laughed, that charming little imp. But I warned him, "I'm serious." So the next time it happened, in Orlando, I got off the plane, looked around for him, went to baggage claim, checked the curb, looked at my phone, walked back inside to the ticket counters, bought a new one-way return ticket, and flew back to Detroit. That was the last time he wasn't at the airport to meet me when I landed.

"I remember," I whispered back.

"Sorry, mama," he said.

It was the first he'd ever sincerely apologized to me. The only time.

And then he was gone. Forever.

I lifted my head from the keyboard and looked at my reflection in the screen. There were new lines on my face from the indentations of the keys…and from grief. This was really happening. I already knew what was coming, and the rest of the world soon would: Hector Camacho is dead.

* * * * *

We're finally moving toward the runway, so I should put this laptop away. Soon we'll lift off the ground. "Slip the surly bonds of earth," as the poet said. I'll hold my breath when I feel the plane bouncing and vibrating, as the flaps slowly retract and the wheels wrestle their way into resting place, as the engines fight against gravity. I'll stare out the window and try to hold it together, try not to envision pallbearers lowering his body into the earth. And eventually, I'll have to come back to earth. I'll flinch at the screech of rubber hitting the runway and close my eyes as we taxi to the gate.

And when my feet finally touch New York, he won't be there to meet me.

He'll be in the Bronx…in a box.

# CHAPTER 1

I met Hector "Macho" Camacho at the beginning of my second life, having spent my first life learning how to live. The years leading up to meeting him are as important to our story as those I spent with him, because they shaped me into a person open enough to fall in love with him, patient enough to sustain our relationship, and strong enough to keep from losing myself along the way.

I began my first life smack in the middle of a ten-piece family. We were, like Ford's Model T, all-American and made in Michigan. I grew up near Lake Erie with seven brothers and sisters, a regular *Brady Bunch*. Actually, the *Partridge Family* might be a better comparison: My dad had bought a big old bus and installed homemade bunk beds. We would all pile into it for family vacations, and in my naive mind, it really did seem like we were living within the confines of a console television set. My father, the patriarch, had driven the same milk delivery route as his father before him—and eventually went to work for Ford. My mother was the most beautiful woman I have ever seen, and my father worshipped her, at least for a while. My life didn't diverge from this picturesque vision of family until I was twelve, when it turned out that, unlike the durable Model T, our family was ultimately unable to weather the rocky road.

I don't know when it started, but I remember the day I first felt my life shifting. It was Halloween, and my parents were taking us to see a house they had bought for us in Estral Beach. We had moved around a lot, but this was the move that really seemed to change things. The fog was thick, so thick I could barely make out the few scattered houses along the two-mile stretch of road to our new home. That seemed like an omen to me, even at the time. When I remember this drive, knowing now what it ultimately meant for my family, the *Twilight Zone* theme plays in my head, muffled slightly by the heavy coastal air. It was here, in Estral Beach, that I started to notice my family falling apart.

As its members left to deal with their own respective problems, it became clear to me that the family, as a whole, was becoming less than the sum of its parts. Before I knew what had hit me, my parents were in divorce court, where my dad was awarded custody of the four youngest siblings and the rest of us were ordered to live with my mom. It wasn't long though before I found myself alone with my mother: my two older sisters were both pregnant and living with their respective boyfriends, my brother was living out of his car, and my mother was only half present, having been diagnosed with bipolar disorder. I was fourteen years old when I realized I would have to ask my father if I could live with him. It was excruciating to think of leaving my mother in her great need, but I had to face that I couldn't live in a house with no heat, no electricity (she wasn't functional enough to pay the bills), and very little food. And it was even more painful that my father needed some convincing. He finally agreed to take me in on the condition that I get a job to provide for myself. Shortly afterward, my mother, unable to care for herself, moved to Taylor to live with my grandmother.

A year later, my four younger siblings and I moved to Dearborn Heights with my father's new family—which included his new wife, Barb, and her own five children—where I began attending my first integrated high school. I worked at McDonald's on weekends to pay for my own food and clothes. I did poorly in school, but my grades didn't reflect it, most likely because I didn't look like a teenager, which meant teachers allowed me to scrape by on minimal effort and mediocre work. In fact, one teacher took his favoritism even further and claimed to be in love with me. At the time, I was happy to receive preferential treatment for my looks, but in hindsight, I wish I hadn't been robbed of a decent education. Still, I was the first of my siblings to graduate high school, and having my father in attendance at my graduation might be the only happy memory I have from that period of my life. I was beginning to believe I just might be able to make something of my life.

Then I met Samade.

Before graduating, I had moved out of my father's house and into my older sister Ila's small two-bedroom home with her husband, their new baby, and our younger sister Colleen. I lived there for my entire senior year of high school. Ila took us in despite having her own family, her own struggles, and very little room. With parents either unwilling or unable to care for their own children, having an older sister who would help in whatever she could made all the difference in the world.

After graduation, I would visit my sister Renee in Detroit. She had two children, and I would stay at their place to watch the kids when she would leave town for several days at a time. Also in that building, in the only other apartment, lived my cousin Tony and her husband. Tony's husband would host regular poker games, which was how I met Samade. One night the boys were playing poker in Tony's apartment while I was babysitting at Renee's. Samade had called for a cab, and when it arrived, I knocked on their door to let him know. He took one look at me and, he says, fell in love.

Samade was ten years older than me, and at first, I had no interest in his advances. He asked my cousin for my number, and I was resistant. Since childhood, I had yet to experience any kind of substantial emotions because my focus in life had been survival. It was like I was surrounded by that same thick fog that had a strangle hold on Estral Beach. I moved through the haze by going through the necessary motions, but I felt nothing. Try as he might, Samade could not cut through the fog. However, my cousins and my sister did not share my hesitation. Eventually, they talked me into agreeing to a date.

We went out once, then another time. A few dates turned into many, and before I knew it, we were going out regularly enough that Samade started being possessive when we were out together. If another man approached me in a bar, Samade would knock him unconscious before he could get a word out. Samade would grab my hand, and we would be running from the bar before I could even comprehend what was happening.

Samade was a complicated man. That much I knew from first meeting him. It was when we were driving home from dinner one night that the storm I saw brewing erupted fully.

Samade was high on coke—or was it speed?—at the time. He was big and bold and liked to live dangerously. Even a fool could see that. But maybe I was the fool who was rapt and fascinated by it. In the frenzy of his drug high, we never made it to dinner that night. Instead, Samade decided to drive to Florida.

To be honest, it was thrilling. The man was so unpredictable and full of life. Once we made it to Florida, he bought me some new clothes and a bathing suit. In my heart of hearts, I hoped that I'd be starting my life over from scratch. We stayed in Florida for over a week, and I can honestly say that much of it was a blur of sunshine, the sea, and Samade vacillating back and forth between being out of his mind and totally down to earth. Who was this man? I was always guessing.

It was when we were driving back through Ohio that he finally let me take the wheel. Maybe he was tired, or maybe he was giving me the feeling of being in the driver's seat for once. It was dark, and I couldn't see a thing. More specifically, I couldn't see the truck driver that was trying to get my attention from inside his towering cabin.

To this day, I don't know why the truck driver was honking. I thought it was because Samade was asleep, but I was the one driving!

It was innocent and strange, but when we finally got back to the house after the long journey, Samade was absolutely livid. He accused me of flirting with the truck driver and trying to lead him on. I couldn't understand how that could be because it was too dark to flirt with anyone.

That was the night I took my first beating. He hit me so hard I saw stars. For a fleeting moment, I understood what it was like to be a boxer—only it was going to be me who would take all the punches for quite some time. I was left on the curb, clutching myself in my ripped clothes. I was crying and confused, battered and beaten. I have to say, it was my first knockout.

As the weeks went by, he was calling me as feverishly as he had beaten me. I wouldn't accept his phone calls, thinking that was the best approach, but it only made it worse. In hindsight, this is classic abusive behavior, and I fell into it hook, line, and sinker.

My sisters Laura and Dana couldn't understand why I kept refusing his calls. To them, he was something glamorous, sexy, and powerful. But I had already seen the dark underbelly. Looking back, it made sense that Samade bought my sisters coats and took them to fancy places. He was spoiling them. He was gaining their consent.

For irrational reasons, I finally relented. He apologized profusely and promised he'd never do it again. God help me, I believed him. Even more painful to think of, I missed him.

I started staying with him at his parents' house, and I was even working at his father's restaurant. I was being immersed into his world. Often, Samade would leave spur of the moment, without saying where he was going. On several occasions, he would lock me in the bedroom from the outside when he was gone. He was beginning to control my whole life, one element at a time. The process was so gradual I couldn't even think to escape. In fact, Samade was becoming my life. And I was beginning to forget what life was like before him.

In hindsight, it makes perfect sense that I gave in. I was getting no attention at home. When I was with Samade, I was somebody. I was important. He would buy me food and clothes, and it's hard to admit, but back then, that constituted spoiling me. It's funny what ends up seeming extraordinary when you have nothing. And to be honest, he could be really romantic. We went to Niagara Falls, somewhere I had always wanted to go. It was famous as a honeymooner's retreat, and I never thought I would make it there with someone. It was absolutely beautiful, and we had an amazing time. I'll never forget the rush that I felt there.

But everything changed on the way home. What was it about Samade going crazy every time he was drawing back to where he came from?

We stopped in a small pizzeria. I spotted these three Nigerian guys sitting across from our booth. I was starved, and the smell of pizza was enticing, but my stomach flipped. I could sense something was about to go very wrong. The pizza finally arrived, but my appetite did not. I could feel that the men were looking at me. And I knew that Samade saw it.

He went completely nuts.

"Hey, stop looking at her!" Samade barked.

"I can look, man. I got eyes. God gave me eyes so I can see."

The temperature in the room shot up several degrees. Samade got up from his seat, and the three Nigerians followed his lead. Suddenly, two of them charged at Samade. He instantly knocked one out then the other and watched as the third guy ran away. Samade opened his wallet, grabbed a fifty-dollar bill, and threw it onto the table. He grabbed me by the arm and pulled me from the pizzeria, leaving bruises that lasted for weeks. He pushed me into the car and drove away from there like criminal being chased by the police. I knew the Nigerians weren't the only ones who would pay for this confrontation; I would pay as well.

I was beginning to recognize a dangerous cycle: I got the shit beat out of me then fled. Samade relented and tried to get me back. I resisted him for a while, and then, I'm humiliated to admit, I would finally relent. I would always give in. I felt powerless and alone.

Don't judge me. When Samade tried to make up for his bad behavior, he was as charming as a man could be, like a knight in shining armor. He was generous and apologetic and looked at me like I was a treasure. I could never resist. This time, Samade promised to never hit me again. I believed him. Completely. There was something in his eyes that I couldn't help believing. Besides, I didn't know how I would live without him. He had convinced me I had no worth.

So I relented. Again. We got our own apartment, and Samade promised he would quit doing drugs. He worked the midnight shift at his cousin's gas station, and we lived in his cousin's apartment building. I would go to work with him. He would sleep on a lounge chair, and I would work his shift so he could get off the pills. Much to my amazement, he finally did.

Our future started to look more hopeful. Samade had saved some money, and he bought a gas station with his cousin. For a while, things got steadily better, though by this time, I had no contact with my family. Not surprisingly, that was how Samade wanted it.

We talked about having children, but by this time, I was "older and wiser"—though I was still only twenty—so, naturally, I was hesitant. Still, I was afraid to refuse Samade because I had nowhere to go. I told him I wanted to go to college before we had children, but he dismissed the idea outright without ever really considering it. We fought about children daily, and the next thing I knew, I was pregnant and, as always, resigned to my fate. I could hear my father's voice saying, "You made your bed. Lie in it."

So I resolved to be the best mom I could be, make the best home I could make, for my child. And at first, things were looking up. Samade was off speed, so he was a lot calmer, and he spent every minute with me, which made me excited about having our second baby. Samade wanted to marry me, but I refused. He was adamant ("My child is not going to be a bastard"), so we compromised and got married in an Arabic ceremony.

During my first pregnancy, I gained almost eighty pounds, which delighted Samade. He would call me "fat ass" and "chubby," and the joy this gave him helped me understand him better. He felt safer now that he thought I was no longer attractive to other men. He would laugh with such glee when he insulted me. Often, he would apologize, saying, "I'm just joking," but I knew he wasn't. I remember sobbing on my twenty-first birthday because I was pregnant and felt so unattractive, trapped in an unhealthy relationship with an abusive and unpredictable maniac.

Ten days later, on July 28, 1984, after fourteen hours of hard labor, my first child, a son, was delivered by C-section: Erick, named after my eldest brother. I fell instantly in love with my baby boy, and Samade was ecstatic. He had a son—Erick's Arabic name is Mustafa—and in his culture, that meant everything.

I was nervous though. There are some moments in life you're never really ready for, and this seemed like one of those times to me. I remember crying at the hospital when it was time to go home. I could not believe they were actually going to send him home with me. I had no experience, I kept telling them. But I learned, of course. I spent all my time joyfully consumed by my new role: mother.

For a while, Samade and I were getting along so well I began to wonder if our relationship might actually work. But then I started losing weight, and Samade started getting violent again, like he was regressing. One night we went to dinner at his cousin's house with several other couples. Naturally, I joined in on the conversation, not knowing every word I said was rubbing Samade the wrong way. When we got home, he lost control, yelling at me, calling me stupid.

"Don't ever open your mouth again. You embarrass me."

So much for this working out. And it only got worse. A year later, I was pregnant again. Samade had persuaded me that Erick needed a friend and that it would "be different this time," promising me he would be a more active, more helpful parent, a real partner. He was so persistent I finally gave in to him. Once again.

I was so happy when our second son, Johnie (Hassan), was born, and Samade was on top of the world. But our euphoria didn't last long. I hardly ever saw my family because Samade wouldn't allow it, and I couldn't go anywhere without the boys because Samade got violently jealous and possessive if I was out in public without them. We almost never had sex, and when I tried to dress provocatively, he would laugh. "You're a mother now. Stop all that bullshit." Of course, the emotional, psychological barbs kept flying. Every chance he got, he put me in my place.

Financial pressures fueled the fire of our discord. Our gas station was losing money, so we sold it on a land contract and bought a neighborhood bar and a three-family house right across the street from the bar. We would send the boys to their *sitto* (grandmother), Samade's mother, so we could both pull shifts at the bar.

As I should have expected, Samade never helped with caring for the boys. When one of them needed something, day or night, he would kick me (literally) out of the bed. "Get your lazy ass up and take care of the kids." I was so unhappy in this relationship but so in love with being a mother. I poured everything I had, all my energy and all my love, into my two sons.

Before long, the bar was doing well, and Samade decided he wanted another child. He harassed me daily, using various abusive tactics. He would degrade me, threaten me, try to make me feel guilty, and entice me with the promise of a daughter, because he knew I wanted a little girl. Eventually, you guessed it, I acquiesced. Nikolas (Samir) was born in January of 1991, and finally, the fog around me started to lift.

Samade's abuse, during and after the pregnancy, was incessant: "You're fat," "You're old," "You're ugly," "No one is going to want you." I heard those words on a daily basis. He built a privacy fence around the house and strictly forbade me from opening the blinds. We rarely had sex and almost never went out. When we were in the car, I had to be careful to look straight ahead. I once yawned in the car, and Samade punched me, yelling, "Stop showing that guy how big your mouth is!" I spent most of my time in the state of fight or flight.

One Friday night, Samade and I left my sister Laura in charge of the bar and went to a local hangout with several couples. After we had been sitting there for a while, I excused myself to go to the bathroom. When I came back to the table, Samade was standing, waiting for me, and I saw that familiar rage in his eyes. He grabbed me by my hair, yelling at me and calling me a whore, and accused me of having fucked a stranger in the bathroom. Mind you, I had only been gone for two minutes, but Samade's anger was never rational. He beat me up, dropped me off at the house, and then returned to spend the rest of the night with our friends.

Things got worse and worse. He started tracking my receipts, even though I always took all three boys everywhere I went. He installed cameras in the bar and watched me all day. When I would come home, he would question my every move. When I worked at night and he was across the street, he would storm into the bar, drag me out, throw me against the wall, and start accusing me. Who had I been talking to? What had I said? He would send me home and then make me return to the bar to work a few minutes later. None of it made any sense.

I began to fear for my sanity and felt depressed. I would lie in bed and pray to God to kill me. I repeatedly told Samade I wanted a divorce, but he would laugh at me, saying, "You're not going anywhere. Nobody wants you. You're old, fat, and ugly. You've got three children." I remember thinking that living on the streets had to be better than what I was enduring.

By the time Nik came along, Samade had allotted me only one hour per day to myself. I could either read or go for a run, but not both. In hindsight, I believe those daily runs saved my life. They were like meditation to me, the only time I could clear my head.

Then I turned thirty, and something inside me snapped. I was lying in bed, depressed, unable to get up, and I resolved to change my life. I asked Samade for a divorce for the hundredth time, and he dismissed me as usual. But this time, I held strong.

I'll never forget the event that put me over the edge, gave me the strength to leave. One day, when Samade was at the bar, Renee came over to our house with her daughter. We went to McDonald's, bought Happy Meals, and returned to our place to have a picnic on the living room floor. Samade called and asked for something, but I couldn't understand what he was saying because the bar was loud. The next thing I knew, he stormed in the front door with that fire.

"You want to fuck with me? You want to fuck with me? Because your sister is here, you think I won't do anything?" he shouted.

Renee and I were dumbfounded, and the kids were terrified. He grabbed me by the hair, carried me to the bedroom, and started punching me. Erick ran after us, crying. "Please don't hit her, Baba! Please stop!" Samade slowly turned to him menacingly.

"Shut the fuck up before I beat the fuck out of you too."

That was it. I was finally finished. I would not back down; I would not give in. He tried everything he could: he ignored me for months, he cut off my money, and he moved upstairs, tapped my phone, and threatened me on a daily basis. But I would never go back. I was finally resolved. And I would soon be free of him, free from this abuse.

I started living my own life. I went for a long run every day and started taking better care of myself, doing whatever I could to get back in shape. The more he called me fat and ugly, the harder I worked. One day I went out to lunch with the owner of the tanning salon I sometimes visited. I was terrified Samade would find out, and I told my new friend I didn't think it was a good idea to see each other again. He grabbed me and kissed me, and for the first time in my life, I felt alive. I realized then and there I had been in a fog, like the one at Estral Beach, my whole life, trying to live unnoticed at my dad's house and then trying to stay alive under the same roof as Samade.

It was the last straw for Samade too. When he found out, from a friend, that I'd been seen with another man, he stole up behind me as I was paying bills, sitting at the dining room table, and punched me in the back of the head, knocking me to the ground. While I was on the floor, he kicked me, called me a whore, spit on me, and screamed, "You want a divorce? You got it!" I ran out of the house and slept in the park that night. I had never felt so alone. I couldn't call my sisters or anyone else in my family; I had let Samade chase my family away.

I gave Samade everything in the divorce, except for custody of the boys. For me, that was the one nonnegotiable item. I worked three jobs, as a server and in real estate, and somehow managed to buy a rundown house. I signed the loan documents on the trunk of the mortgage officer's car, eager to start my new life. My brother-in-law helped with all the repairs the house needed, and I started reconnecting with my family.

One day I walked into the office of a mortgage company because I wanted to refinance my house. There was a beautiful man named Peter standing behind one of the desks. I couldn't take my eyes off him. The most amazing thing about my attraction to him is this: he was the same person who had given me the original loan. I had signed the documents on Peter's trunk, but I hadn't even noticed him that day. Now I couldn't *not* notice him. The fog was truly lifting.

A few minutes after I left the office (reluctantly!), Peter called to offer me a job as his assistant. I was hesitant but eventually accepted, because it was a great job with benefits, which allowed me to quit my other jobs. I was so attracted to Peter though that it was hard to concentrate on learning the ropes, and I found the mortgage business difficult to comprehend. I would stay up late, studying and crying, but I vowed to never give up. One night I woke from a dead sleep, sat straight up in my bed, and affirmed, "I got this." I had finally found my calling: I was a natural-born saleswoman.

Six months later, Peter resigned. But I had found my footing by then. I had found my way.

That was when I met Hector.

# CHAPTER 2

Hector Luis Camacho Matias was born on May 24, 1962. He was the first son of Maria Esther Matias and Hector Luis Camacho, born at his grandmother's house in Toa Baja, Puerto Rico. Hector had an older sister named Raquel and, later, a younger brother named Felix.

He was only three or four when his mother packed up and left Hector Sr. She took the kids to New York, where they lived in various housing projects. It was common for these dumps to be lacking in heat and water. The little family lived in one- or two-bedroom units. They kept moving. Do you blame them?

Maria met a new guy named Rueben. She would eventually have two more children with him, Estralla and Esther. That totaled up to five children in all.

For whatever reason, Hector loved to dress up in suits even at a young age. I remember being told about the day that Hector got in a bad fight and ripped the back of his suit jacket. They sent him home to his mother, and he was furious, scared, and confused by what he had done. This was just the start of what would be his problematic behavior. He was kicked out of almost every Catholic school in New York. The young rebel in him came from an unknown place, but that archetype would continue to drive his life.

It was when he was living on 112th Street and Lexington that a big electrical fire erupted in his apartment. The family was terrified. Yelling, screaming, and crying could be heard amid the blaze. I have a feeling that it didn't frighten Hector at all. Such chaos was innate to him. He was not the calm amid the storm. He was the storm amid the storm.

The electrical fire led to another move, of course. This time, it was in Spanish Harlem. More specifically, the James Weldon Johnson Projects.

Many of those characteristics that Hector had as a boy were still there as a man: hyperactivity, getting on people's nerves, and aggression. Maria dutifully made her pilgrimage to the principal's office to pick him up each time he got kicked out of school. But in grade school, Hector had the good fortune to meet two of his lifelong friends, Edwin and Tito. They were with him at the beginning, and they'd be with him at the end.

By the age of nine, Hector was sneaking out of the family apartment down the fire escape, and he would ride the subway back and forth. Hector would go farther and farther each time. What was all that endless wandering about? In hindsight, I think that his restlessness drove him to do a lot of things.

By this same age, he had made his own roller skates out of cowboy boots and metal skate blades. Wearing these skates, he would jump cars and head uptown. The skates also provided a great getaway for looting stores and making a clean escape. He even once jumped a bus and rode it onto the highway. He clung on for dear life while his homemade roller skates were unravelling at his feet. Sparks were flying! People in their cars were screaming at the bus, trying to get the bus driver to see what was going on. Once the driver finally noticed, he stopped the bus. Hector unlaced his skates and made a dash for it. He rode home on the subway in his socks. This was just the beginning of Hector's illustrious stealing career.

He would go to Gimbels and hide in the racks till the store closed. Once the coast was clear, he'd bag up whatever caught his eye and then hide in the trash bins, waiting to be wheeled out in the morning, leaving him free to return home. In his bag of goodies? Often G.I. Joe.

Hector loved his G.I. Joes as a kid. He'd recreate gang wars with them when he was confined to his room, which was often. His thirty Joes created quite the gang war. One day his mother saw his bounty of toys and started yelling and crying in Spanish. She was no fool. She threw them in the incinerator.

Hector was always one to have his way. The very next day, he was back at Gimbels, replacing all his G.I. Joes and adding a heavy arsenal of airplanes and helicopters. That was one-upmanship at its best.

Hector liked to pick on older kids. It makes me laugh to think of it. What kind of kid likes to pick on older kids? But that was pure Hector. There was one older boy who got so fed up that he threatened retaliation. Hector became frightened, confused by his own inclinations, and so he ran home. He had toyed with the devil, and the devil toyed back. Funny enough, when he arrived home, his mother told him to get his ass back out there and finish what he started.

"If you don't, you'll have me to deal with," Maria had said.

When it came to dealing with the opponent's wrath or his mother's wrath, he chose the former. So he went back and kicked the guy's ass. That was how it all started. I'm convinced. Many more fights were to come. And you know something? He would win most of them. He fought often and won often. Sometimes he'd employ a brick or a bat. If it meant that he had the upper hand, he'd use it. It was less threatening than going home to Maria.

That being said, Maria had her merits. She kept Hector out of the local gangs, which most of his friends had already joined by the age of twelve. Hector and his boys, Edwin and Tito, would hang out in the Jefferson Projects, a shotgun ready for action in Hector's bag. He was known as Little Man. And for a little guy, he packed quite a punch. Everyone knew that he was a badass kid.

Rueben would take Hector to Connie's gym, where he discovered his love of karate. It didn't take long before Hector was a black belt. When he became focused on something, he quickly mastered it. He was obsessed with Bruce Lee, Elvis Presley, and even Michael Jackson! On the roof of the projects, he'd practice his karate, jumping from roof to roof, kicking and fighting the air.

Robert Velez was an ex-gang member who Hector met at the gym. It was Velez who got Hector into boxing. It wasn't long before

Hector gravitated toward new friends, Sammy Tirado and Mickey Goodwin, fellow boxers and badasses.

Hector was starting to blossom by age fifteen. He was learning to read, enrolled in Manhattan High School for troubled kids, and he stumbled upon the man who would become his mentor and father figure. He won his first Golden Gloves competition. Sure, he was arrested for the first time too, but for the most part, things were coming into focus.

Patrick Flannery was Hector's language arts teacher. He was responsible for teaching Hector how to read while also providing guidance and support. Hector was an incredibly smart kid when he was given the right encouragement and support, and Flannery did just that. Hector was obsessed with writing stories about boxing and even wrote about how he'd one day become a world champion, buying a house for his mother. Even though Flannery did not want Hector to box, thinking that he had too much potential to broaden his mind, Hector persisted anyway.

Flannery bought Hector his first pair of boxing shoes and signed him up for the Golden Gloves. When Hector was told that he was too young, a fake birth certificate was produced. He was always resourceful. And when he didn't make the weight for his first fight, he shaved his head bald and was just able to make it. He was the youngest Golden Gloves champion in history, mostly thanks to the fact that no one knew how young he really was! And he was also a tremendous fighter even then. It was Flannery who gave Hector his nickname "Macho" Camacho, even though others were shooting for Hector "Piaso," which means "clown" in Spanish.

Despite these successes, Hector landed in jail twice. He had a thing for stealing cars, borrowing them for a couple of days, then cleaning them up and returning them. The first time he went to jail, it was for stealing a car. The police managed to chase him for thirty blocks and finally cornered him in an alley. Hector became trapped on the driver's side and managed to crawl through the passenger's side before they caught him. Then he had a nice little vacation at Rikers Island, thirty stitches in his face. It was one stitch for every block that the cops chased him.

It wasn't long before Hector was out again, roller skating and dancing his way through Harlem. This was when he met Myra, who would become the mother to his child Hector Jr. Myra was in a gang at the time, which Hector had still managed to avoid.

It wasn't long before Myra was pregnant, and Hector was back in jail. He was with a friend, stealing a car, when his friend stabbed the driver of the said car. It earned Hector a ticket back to Rikers. But this time, things were a little different. He was getting into tons of fights in jail and found himself sent to solitary confinement. No blanket, no heat, no TV. Hector would recall hearing the radio through the walls, and whenever the song "Street Life" came on, he would start to cry. He began talking to himself and even prayed to God to let him out. He wanted another chance. He deserved one.

And to be fair, Hector did want to become a better person. He wanted to see his beloved mother again and his future son.

Standing before the judge, Hector swore that he had learned his lesson. He also mentioned that if they let him out, he'd become a world champion in boxing. That was exactly what he did.

Amazingly, the judge let him go, and Hector would go on to win two more Golden Glove championships, making it three in total. No boxer of Hector's young age had ever achieved that. He was the first Puerto Rican to win Golden Gloves and world champion.

Finally free from doing prison time, Hector was able to spend father time with Hector Jr. But it wasn't all fun and games. When Hector became overwhelmed and didn't know how to parent, he admitted to locking Junior in the closet. He also wanted Junior to be tough, like he was. He'd pay kids to follow him home from school and pick a fight with him. Aside from this vicious behavior, there was the flip side. Hector sometimes enjoyed playing the part of a goofy dad. At one of Junior's birthday parties, Hector dressed up like Batman and ran around the house, yelling, "I am the Macho Man!" Junior just shook his head and said to the crowd of gathered kids, "That's my dad."

Fierce and fiercely loving, that was Hector.

At heart, Hector was a family man. But he had grown up with so much dysfunction that his methods weren't always ideal.

It wasn't long before Hector got a new manager named Billy Giles. As Hector was quickly getting better and better, he needed someone to take him to the next level, and Billy was the guy. But Billy took Hector to the next level in many regards. He introduced him to cocaine. When they traveled together, Billy would store his cocaine in the dresser. Hector took note. As soon as Billy was gone, Hector would go straight to the dresser and steal it.

"I am the fight maker. You're nothing. You need me," Billy used to tell Hector, keeping him hooked in many respects.

But Billy could be both cruel and kind, something that made a lot of sense to Hector. When he won his first professional fight, Billy bought Hector a triple-black Cadillac Eldorado.

Since he was getting to be quite a big shot, Hector was determined to show it. He had several girlfriends at the same time. Hector had this friend named Scooby. Good ole Scooby liked to go on dates too, so he and Hector would go together. Scooby would take the mother, and Hector would take the daughter. It worked perfectly. It didn't take long before Scooby, a notorious drug dealer, found himself in jail, where he was eventually killed. Such side stories and supporting characters in Hector's life were common. He was always making friends with bad guys who met tragic ends. Hector wouldn't have it any other way.

The girlfriends kept coming, and so did the sex. When Hector would return home to visit his mom and sister, he'd find someone to take with him, and they'd have sex on the roof, in the hallway, anywhere they could find room. We've already established that he was a man of many appetites.

After winning his first professional fight, Billy Giles and Don King sent Hector to Detroit to train at Kronk Gym. His new trainer went by the name of Emanuel Steward. Hector would beat Emanuel's fighters up. This was impressive, to say the least.

Hector would train on Belle Isle, a little island off Detroit. Billy would egg him on, making fun of him, saying, "You see that old man over there? He is the Macho Man, not you." This would piss Macho off so bad he removed all his clothes in the dead of winter and started running naked, screaming, "I am the Macho Man! I am the Macho

Man!" And he wouldn't get back in the car till Billy conceded that he was indeed the Macho Man.

Macho used to stay at the Holiday Inn in Southgate. One night he heard someone stealing his brand-new corvette, so buck naked, he jumped out of bed and started chasing them. The police arrested him until they realized who he was. When Tony and Jerry went to pick him up, he was on a desk in a robe they had found for him, telling stories. He had everyone in tears from laughing.

Hector's star kept rising as his training became more intense and his focus clearer. He finally purchased an apartment in Forest Hills. Would you believe it? Before that, he was living at the Holiday Inn.

Hector even got a steady girlfriend. Her name was Keisha, and Hector was crazy about her. But this didn't mean fidelity. Girls threw themselves at Hector. It was part and parcel of being a big, up-and-coming boxer, and Hector couldn't resist. Too bad, Keisha.

There was the famous Johnny Sato fight in New Jersey, and Hector was up to his usual antics. He did this little dance on the boardwalk that drew a big crowd, maybe more than the fight itself. I wouldn't be surprised if he was yelling "I am the Macho Man," as I know he loved to do. Hector was staying at one of those fancy Trump hotels and often high. He defamed a mural that cost Don King tens of thousands of dollars. Hector couldn't be compelled to care. He was literally living the high life.

Hector ran into Bobby Uketel in Jersey. Bobby was a billionaire from Alaska. Bobby took to Hector so strongly that he arranged a flight for him in his home state. Of course, Hector had to fly his entire entourage on the private plane. The mansion in Alaska turned out to be the perfect place for training, and that was what Hector did.

It wasn't long before Bobby had out with it and admitted that he had a thing for Hector. He wanted to sleep with him. Hector recounted to me humorously.

"Ahhh, Bobby, I don't swing that way, but thanks. We can still be friends." Bobby was dead shortly thereafter. Remember when I mentioned the cruel fate of Hector's friends? It was a brief relationship, but Hector still has the fur coat to prove that it happened.

Hector was still really young at this point. At the age of twenty-one, he won his first world title right in Puerto Rico. A journalist asked him if he was happy, and Hector replied, "I'm twenty-one, wearing leather, and the world champion. I couldn't be happier."

And as things were progressing fast, it was time for yet another trainer. This time, it was Ismael Leandry, who would become a lifelong friend. Leandry convinced Hector that he needed to own two condos in ESJ Towers. It made perfect sense. Hector could keep two or three women in the apartments at all times to cater to his every whim. With a new location came another new friend. This time, it was George Sosa, brother to Jose Sosa. He was Macho's new best friend.

One New Year's Eve, he offered George's wife ten thousand dollars if she would let George go out with him. She said no way. An hour later, when she didn't hear from them, she found them in the back bedroom, shimmying down sheets, trying to sneak out.

With more accomplishments came more cars. Don King bought Hector a shiny, new Lamborghini, which subsequently caught fire on FDR Drive in New York City. Hector would often abandon cars when there was something wrong with them, and he'd just go straight to the dealer to buy a new car. And he'd pay in cash. He was always paying with cash.

Hector was living the dream, and he was bringing Edwin and Tito along for the ride. They'd fly across the country and then drive around in a limo, Hector picking what bar they'd go to first. He loved karaoke bars.

"Stop, that's the bar!" he would say from behind tinted windows. Hector would then get out, run into the bar, grab the mike, and sing "Macho Man"! The crowds would just go crazy. He could always attract a crowd. This was a prime opportunity to pick up girls. And when he got tired of them, he'd pull up to a convenience store and send the girl in for smokes. Once they were in the shop, he'd just leave. One time, he picked up a girl in his jeep at the airport. They got into a bad accident, but still, lying in bed, mangled and torn up, he had sex with her.

One day after training, Macho was lying on the couch. He screamed for me to come lie with him. Hector told me he was offered a part in *West Side Story*. One million dollars was the paycheck. Hector was excited until they informed him that his character would die. He turned it down.

"The Macho Man does not die," he said with childish pride.

Hector was invited to the White House to meet President Reagan. They picked him up in a limo. Upon stepping into the White House, he excused himself and went into the bathroom to do some coke. After taking a couple of bumps of blow and washing his hands, he stepped out to meet the president.

As you can see, Hector was always moving to new places to train and just to move in general. The next big thing was in California. Hector loved California because it was so glamorous. It gave him a chance to show off. CBS invited him six times to appear on TV. He posed for *Playgirl* magazine. He would party at the Playboy mansion and take drugs, allowing himself yet again to relinquish control.

Hector was growing too big for his own breeches. He dropped Billy Giles and Don King. As it turned out, Billy was stealing from him, using Hector's money to pay his taxes. In retaliation, Billy told Hector that he was all washed up. Of course, he was just pissed because he was caught stealing, but the blow still was taken personally by Hector.

As for Don King, he thought that he wasn't being fair.

"I own you as long as you hold the title!" Don fired back.

In response, Hector relinquished his title and told Don King to go fuck himself then went on to win another. Needless to say, he was confident in his abilities.

Despite all this accomplishment and bravado, Hector was depressed. It was the other side of him that no one saw. He took some time off from fighting because of it. The depression would lead him to go to the airport, buy a ticket to wherever he felt like going, and just fly away. No luggage, no itinerary, and no regrets. All he'd bring was a pocket full of cash. He'd find the nearest hotel and get high for a few days, unfamiliar with his surroundings.

Once the depression was at bay, Hector would get to work at promoting himself. He always said that everyone needs a gimmick, so he found a number of outrageous outfits. He'd show up at other people's fights, get in the ring, grab the cards, and prance around like a diva. He'd even call the fighters out and make fun of them to their faces. This gimmick ended up being brilliant and got Hector the attention that he craved.

Despite all this, somewhere deep inside, Hector knew that he was on a path to destruction. He tried something new, built a small training camp in Clewiston, Florida, and tried the simple life. Hector would chop down trees for his workout, and he'd run five miles a day. He found a new friend who had a calming influence. Marty Cohen convinced him to open a retirement fund, telling Hector to "use his head." He was the first to tell Hector that the money wouldn't always be there. Hector took this to heart. He used his head. Not only did he open a retirement fund, he also invested in bonds.

That was when his head cleared, and he got serious about boxing again. But things always seemed to get crazy when he was nurturing the fighter in him.

In 1986, he was arrested for reckless driving, driving without a license, driving an unregistered vehicle, driving without insurance, executing an unsafe lane change, and also having sex while driving.

Go big or go home, right?

In the same year, he was leaving the famous Edwards fight, driving a lotus. It was at an Indian reservation. He was high and drunk and driving fast over a hill when he skidded across the tops of a couple of cars and ended up in a palm tree. Hector managed to climb his way out and down before he realized that he left his championship belt in the car. So he climbed back up and retrieved it. Then he casually walked back to the training camp.

The camp was surrounded by cornfields. This was for protection. He also had a fireman's pole that ran down into the garage and a getaway jeep that was parked farther afield. He used a pair of binoculars to see if the cops had followed him.

Despite these hijinks, Hector's star in the boxing ring just rose and rose. He was a sensation. Hector was also his own promoter and came up with even more outrageous outfits for himself.

He was arrested in Clewiston for threatening a young student with a gun. Why he was doing that is anyone's guess. He received probation by paying a huge fine and then went next door to a bar. He was with a friend at the time. The two of them sat down, ready to make a toast to his victory, when Hector's friend disappeared for about ten minutes. The friend returned to the probation office and stole back Hector's money and then some. Oh, and he decided to start a fire too.

The police weren't far from the perpetrators, so they went next door to the bar. To be honest, the police were fascinated. They were so impressed by Hector's antics that they didn't arrest him but asked for an autograph instead. It wasn't until they were outside that they realized they had both been pickpocketed to boot.

Hector was already making decent money, but that paycheck went sky high after his fight with Ray "Boom Boom" Mancini in 1989. He was still in Clewiston and also had an apartment in Orlando.

All throughout the fight, Hector was nagging Mancini relentlessly, calling him Rayski and yelling, "You're just jealous of me!"

"You'll get yours! You'll see!" Mancini yelled back.

Even though Hector won the match and $1.2 million dollars, he still wasn't satisfied.

"I underestimated him. I didn't train right," he said to his team. He would need to push himself harder.

Another lady came into Hector's life, but this time, she'd stay for a while.

But things weren't always so smooth between the two. Amy would make scenes, become hysterical. But there was still something between them. She got pregnant with her second child, another son, but this time it was Hector's. She gave birth to the child in another training camp and named him Christian.

With a little family forming, it was good that Hector got another million-dollar fight with Julio Cesar Chavez. At the match, he went up behind Chavez on the dais and gave the crowd a thumbs down. This was also to rile up his former trainer, Don King.

He would sometimes strip totally naked for his weigh-ins just to shock people. And his shocking scene at the Miami Airport landed him in jail again. This was in 1992, when he started running around the lobby, yelling, "I am the Macho Man!" When the police tried to quiet him down, he fought back, breaking an officer's leg. He was charged on three counts of assault to an officer, disorderly conduct, and possession of drugs.

More million-dollar fights were on the horizon. He'd fight Felix Trinidad, and he would lose. It almost didn't matter. The money was still great, and he had a huge fan base that filled the arena.

He went through a brief phase of church and rehab. Hector was always vacillating back and forth like that. He married Amy, because it seemed like the right thing to do, especially while he was going through a "good" phase.

I shouldn't have to tell you that this phase didn't last long.

The good news was that he was fighting a lot. This kept Hector reasonably out of trouble. He was set for at least another twenty fights. He would travel to New York, Las Vegas, all across the country. And of course, he was still training in Florida. Hector had a thing for Florida.

Macho was a natural-born salesman. He believed in himself, and his mouth was more his weapon than his fist. He drew media attention everywhere he went. His split curl, fancy costumes, and flamboyancy made him an entertaining showman. In a flurry of hand-and-speed style, Macho could overwhelm his opponent, and he gained audiences around the world. He had been known for hitting his opponents then spinning them around and whacking them on the head.

His ten most memorable fights are as follows:

*Perry Ballard (Houston Texas)*. Macho fought with him for his tenth world championship belt. He trained with the legendry Angelo Dundee.

*Sugar Ray Leonard.* Leonard chose Macho for his last fight. Big mistake. They went everywhere promoting this fight, shaking hands, and trading barbs, but when it came down to fight day, Macho was five hours late. He was driving in with his entourage and wouldn't go to the weigh-in till they fed him. He kept everyone waiting. When Sugar Ray came up to shake his hand before the fight, Macho smacked his hands away, saying, "We aren't friends, motherfucker. I am going to kick your ass."

*Greg Haugen.* Macho suffered his first defeat at the hands of Haugen only because of his arrogance. He refused to touch gloves before the fight. Haugen later tested positive for illegal substance, and a rematch was ordered, which Macho won hands down.

*Roberto Duran.* Macho was thirty-four; Duran, forty-five. Macho went toe to toe with the "Hand of Stone," but he couldn't touch Macho. He was way too quick and outboxed him. They would have a rematch in 2001, which Macho won by unanimous decision. The fight became famous because Hector literally kicked the living daylights out of him.

*Vinny Pazienza.* Pazienza fought dirty using his head and elbows, but Macho, being a slicker fighter, outboxed him. He had to. He talked way too much shit before the fight, and he had to back it up with his fists.

*Julio Cesar Chavez.* Macho thought this was the time for people to start taking him seriously as a fighter, but no matter how much he tried to make something happen, he couldn't. Chavez was a bigger, better fighter. He made a ton of money on this fight, which helped him deal with the loss.

*Ray "Boom Boom" Mancini.* Macho taunted Ray relentlessly before the fight, calling him a girl and Rayski. He played with his mind, using his mouth as his weapon, saying everything he could do to get on his nerves. It worked. Macho beat Ray pound for pound; he was just the better fighter.

*Oscar De La Hoya.* This was one of Macho's highest-paying fights. He got over three million dollars. There was a side bet: if Oscar knocked Macho out, he would pay him a million dollars and he could cut off Macho's famous spit curl. Oscar went on to win the fight, but because he didn't knock Macho out, there was no million dollars or cutting of Macho's curl.

*Johnny Sato.* Before the fight, Macho did a dance on the New Jersey boardwalk, which drew a bigger crowd than the fight. After the fight, Macho stayed at the Trump Hotel. There was a beautiful mural on the ceiling. He was smoking a joint and decided he was going to put a curl on the mural. He couldn't reach it, so he stacked some tables and chairs together, climbed up, and drew a curl on the mural. When Don King found out, he was so furious, but Macho just blamed it on his entourage. This fight also landed him a space on the cover of *Sports Illustrated*.

*Rafael Limon.* They called him bazooka. He was supposed to blow Macho away. Macho was at the top of his game and blew Limon away in the fifth round; he was unstoppable. He won his first world title with this fight.

*Edwin Rosario.* The most controversial fight and the fight that changed Macho's fighting for the worst was Edwin Rosario. Macho sent Edwin a pair of red panties and his autograph. He paid a kid off the street twenty dollars to deliver them to Rosario and say it was from the governor of Puerto Rico. He paid the kid another twenty to stay there and watch his face and report back to him how it went. Macho later said that that backfired on him; he underestimated Rosario. After that, Macho never fought the same again.

It was also around this time that Hector was trying to escape Amy. He always had this need to escape, and it led him to do strange things. I remember this story where Hector decided to lock himself in a men's bathroom and hold all its inhabitants hostage while he snorted coke. He thought the whole thing was a blast. He kept snorting, telling jokes, walking around like he owned the place and all the guys inside. When one man tried to escape, Hector gave him a big smile and said, "I don't think so." Hector got away with this terrifying behavior because he was the Macho Man after all.

More offers were coming in for TV appearances, and Hector loved this. He'd go anywhere where he had an audience. This time, it was for the *Wayans Bros.* show in LA. Hector was going to play "Hot Pepper" Lopez.

It was finally in 1999 that Amy put out a restraining order against Hector. When he came home, he was none too pleased and was eventually arrested and charged for breaking the garage door down.

But as it turned out, Hector was done with Amy anyway. He just couldn't stand to have a door closed on him no matter who did the closing. But where one door closes, another opens, as they say. Behind the next door that opened, there would be me.

# CHAPTER 3

I'll never forget the first time I met Hector. I was working for Long Beach Mortgage. Long hours and demanding clients were taking their toll. That was why it came as a welcome surprise when my dear friends Tina and Ramsey, also mortgage brokers, offered to take me with them to Canada. They had VIP tickets to a special fight at the Windsor Casino, and it was invite-only. Not only that but it was also last minute.

It was late on a Friday night, and they were packing their bags.

It seemed crazy to do something so last minute! But it felt good to be impulsive for once. Still, they needed to talk me into it a bit, and by the time they were done describing the destination, I was rushing home to pack my bags too. I changed into a tight little black dress with tall black patent high heels. The three of us piled into Ramsey's truck, full of anticipation and excitement.

The drive from Detroit didn't take long. We arrived at the casino and pulled into the valet. The host approached. I could tell that he took an instant liking to me because he gave me a little wink. Maybe it was the black dress. The host was in charge of showing us around. He even took us inside to where the event was to take place. Tina and Ramsey sat down in the front-row seats, and the host kept showing things.

"This is Hector 'Macho' Camacho," the guy said with pride.

I was not a boxing fan, so I had no idea at the time who Hector was. Hector smiled, and there was a little glint in his eye. There was attraction for sure…and a little danger. We shook hands, and that was that.

Tina, Ramsey, and I watched the main event from the front row. It was a four-round flight, I recall. When the announcer introduced Hector, he stepped into the ring wearing a crown, and he strutted around the ring like he owned the place. He was making a special appearance.

Again, I knew nothing about boxing, but I knew enough to see that Hector was an extraordinary man. He was powerful, and his body was sculpted. I hate to admit it, but I was impressed.

We got invited to the VIP after-party up in the private area. The three of us walked in, and Hector was sitting in the corner by the window all by himself. It was strange actually. We sent him a vodka and orange juice from the bar. We enjoyed our drinks and didn't hear anything back from Hector, so we decided that it was time to leave. As we were walking toward the elevator, someone bumped into me. When I turned around, it was him.

"Excuse me, I think you bumped into me," Hector said.

"No, I think you bumped into me," I replied.

I kept walking, but I could feel his eyes on me. Finally, he hopped into the elevator with us.

"You wanna go gambling downstairs?" he asked me casually. Tina and Ramsey looked at me in shock.

"No, thanks. I'm good," I replied, not being a gambler.

"You want to have a drink with me later?" Hector asked, not letting up.

I looked to my friends, and they both agreed that I should go. They were going to gamble a bit, and Tina said she'd come meet us at the bar later.

So I went.

Hector and I stood at the bar and ordered some drinks. Just then, the host from earlier walked past. He didn't seem too happy to see me with Hector. Maybe he knew something that I did not know. At the time, I didn't pay it a second thought.

I was amazed by how surprising Hector was on that first encounter. He was shy and cute. Boyish, I would say. Even humble. He had this remarkable smile and fabulous charisma. We talked for twenty minutes or so till my friends found us and said they were ready to leave.

Hector escorted us to the valet.

"You wanna come upstairs for a grilled cheese sandwich?" he asked. I could tell he didn't want me to go. I had to laugh.

"I'm good, thank you. I gotta go," I replied, motioning to my friends.

Tina and Ramsey jumped in the truck, and we exchanged phone numbers. Hector gave me that boyish smile again, and I think that those drinks had gone to my head. I didn't want to leave, but I knew I couldn't stay. My heart fluttered, and I leaned over and gave Hector a kiss! He stood there and smiled as I walked away.

When I got to the truck, I turned back to look at him, and he still stood there with a big ole smile on his face. I waved goodbye and got in the truck. I wasn't sure I'd ever see him again.

A few days passed, and I didn't hear from Hector. I assumed it was just a one-time thing. He probably had other girls who were waiting to hear from him too.

But then I got a call from the Windsor Police Station. It was Hector. He asked if I'd come pick him up. He said it was my fault anyhow.

My heart sank. I had no idea what he was talking about! But he eventually explained that the host who had his eye on me was pissed that I was with Hector, so he called the police. Hector had entered Canada illegally with a felony charge, and the host knew it. Tony and one of his friends brought Macho over on a boat because they couldn't get him through customs.

I asked Hector why it took so long to call me. It had been days! He explained in a rather sweet way that he was catching up on rest and enjoying the quiet in jail. Also, he was hounded for autographs the whole time he was there, something that Hector never shied away from.

"I don't know if you know this, but I'm a little famous," he said to me over the phone.

"Yeah? So am I!" I said with a laugh. The situation was nothing if not odd and funny.

I wanted to drive to pick him up that very minute, but I still had work to do and was running late. We were sponsoring a golf outing that day. But I decided that it was too urgent, and so I left work to get Hector. I called my boss and asked if I could bring a friend to the golf outing.

It was only when my boss asked who it was that I got a hearty *no* in response.

I picked Hector up, and he was just as boyish as the other night and still smiling. I took him to my house so I could change. In my room, I could see Hector outside in the yard, shadowboxing. It was transfixing. I couldn't turn away.

"Ah, Mom, who is that strange man shadowboxing in the yard?" my oldest son asked, and I shook my head in dismay. I started laughing.

"He's just a friend," I replied.

Just then, the phone rang, and it was my boss. It turns out that she had a change of heart. Maybe she consulted her team about it, and now having Hector Camacho at the outing was very much what she wanted.

"We'd love to see him," she said over the phone. There was sarcasm in her voice, like she thought I was lying or something.

When I showed up with Hector, you wouldn't believe the surprise on all their faces. I was driving a triple-black convertible Camaro at the time, so when we pulled up with the top down, we were quite the pair. It was a warm, beautiful night, and I loved the feeling of having Hector by my side. I felt like I had a trophy date!

When we got to the country club, I walked Hector down to the bar and did some preparations on the room. The goal was to accrue some accounts from the event. Every once in a while, I'd go to check on Hector, and of course, he'd be surrounded by a lot of men. The saleswoman in me saw an opportunity. I handed Hector a stack of my cards and told him every time someone approached that he should hand them my card.

When the event was finally over, and a success, I drove home. Hector was going to stay with some Detroit friends of the Villareal family, Tony and Kelly. Seemed like Hector had friends everywhere. When I dropped him off, I came in to meet the family. Considering the strange circumstances under which Hector and I met for the second time, it was funny how casual things were. I felt like I had known Hector for a long time already. I left him there and drove home, unable to shake him from my mind.

Another couple of days went by before he called again. He asked if I would meet him at Tony's house, and I willingly complied. Truth be told, I was excited to see him again. Tony, Kelly, Hector, and I went out to dinner that night. But before we could get out the door, we had to listen to Macho for two hours telling stories in Tony's basement. Hector stood ceremoniously with his leg up on a table, elbow resting on his knee, waving his hands back and forth, up and down, as he held court. We were bursting with laughter. He was always a marvelous storyteller.

We finally got out of the house and went to Simon's in Allen Park and Hockeytown. Hockeytown was a favorite of Hector's, right in Downtown Detroit. It was slow that night. Macho got on stage and sang. In hindsight, of course, he did! But at the time, I was really surprised. He started to sing to me, right at me. I liked it a lot.

Hector acted like someone who couldn't give less of a fuck. The world was his oyster. He was so cool. We stayed for an hour, just slow dancing and looking into each other's eyes. He flashed that beautiful smile at me, and I flashed him mine. It felt nice being that close to him, but it had to come to an end. I took him home and left him with Tony, hoping to hear from him after a few days.

He called me the next day, and I was thrilled. We tried to get into this new bar in Detroit where there was a dress code. Macho had jeans on that night. We asked to talk to the owner, and the minute he came to the door, he recognized me and immediately let us in.

"So you're the celebrity here," he said with a smile. I just laughed it off. He kept insisting that he was the celebrity, but I still wasn't seeing it. He just seemed like some guy I met in Canada.

Finally, after a couple of weeks, I brought Macho to my house to stay over. My kids weren't home then. They had gone to camp in Dearborn with their Uncle Nabil, and Hector and I had not slept together yet. We went to dinner that night by ourselves, and it was really wonderful to be alone with him. We came home and made love all through the night. I'll never forget when he lifted up the sheet that covered me and took his hand, running it up and down my body, and he whispered, "You are my fantasy. I always wanted a beautiful white woman like you."

He thought I was asleep, and I pretended that I was. Finally, he lay down beside me and fell asleep. I woke up that first morning and wanted to go and get us some breakfast. When I was out, the house-phone rang. It was my ex. Hector answered the phone.

"Where's Shelly?" my ex asked, a little perturbed.

"I don't know. She's not here," Hector replied coldly, hanging up the phone. In Hector's defense, he already had the habit of calling me Shirl. It wasn't that he didn't know my name, but he just couldn't pronounce Shelly.

This incensed my ex. He had admitted to me that he still loved me, and I could feel him trying to control my life even then. He called back.

"Listen, what if my kids called and you answered? What would they think?" he demanded.

Hector was nonplussed. He said, "My brother, it's Macho time," and then he hung up again.

My ex went crazy, beeping and calling me. He even called my eldest son.

"Baba, who is this man your mother is dating? I'm going to kick his ass!" he exclaimed.

"Maybe you could. He's kinda short," my son replied, ignorant of who it really was whom I was seeing.

Months later, Hector met my ex at a bar. He stole away to call my son again.

"Baba, you didn't tell me he was a professional boxer! You told me I could kick his ass!"

"Baba, I did not tell you could kick his ass. I told you he was short," my son replied.

It was one of our last nights together. Hector was to leave for a fight, so we went out together, just the two of us. We had a nice, quiet dinner in Detroit. The meal done, we drove down Michigan Avenue. I was behind the wheel, and we pulled over. Leaving the top down, Hector put me in the back seat and sat beside me and made love to me. Hector could be intensely sexy. This kind of sex was innocent in light of what was to come later.

"Do you like me because I'm a boxer?" Hector asked during the drive home. We were both in kind of a hazy glow.

"You're thirtysomething years old. You don't have much boxing left," I said by way of reassurance that it wasn't the boxing I was attracted to. Hector smiled.

"Why do you like me then?" Hector asked.

"I can't lie," I replied. "You're sexy, you're strong, you're single, and you're my age."

Hector's face fell.

"I can't lie either. I am married but separated," he explained. "My wife left for New York. I came to Detroit to be with family," he said. Hector considered the Villareals to be family.

Two days later, I took Hector to the airport. I walked him all the way to the gate. We did not discuss if we would see each other again. I stood there at the gate and watched him walk away, waiting for him to turn around and look at me one last time. At the very last minute, before he boarded, he turned and smiled at me. I smiled back and gave him a little wave.

Much later, he would tell me that he said to himself, *If I turn around and she is still there, we got a chance.*

It was around August that same year when I heard from him again. He called me and told me to come visit him in Puerto Rico. What I didn't know at the time was that Hector had a special travel agent who handled itineraries for all the ladies whom he'd fly out to him, anywhere in the world. Needless to say, I was very naive in the beginning of our relationship. I consulted friends and family who tried to tell me not to go. But I wouldn't be stopped. I didn't listen to anyone. I left my kids with my mom, and Tina drove me to the airport.

Hector's offer was irresistible. He was irresistible. And I was hungry for something more from life.

As soon as I got off the plane, he was waiting for me. Hector grabbed my luggage and drove me to one of his condos at ESJ Towers. I couldn't believe I was seeing him again. I was full of excitement. It was so unlike me to just jump on a plane to Puerto Rico. It was thrilling to do something so unexpected and new. There was not a shroud of worry in my mind.

That first night, we made love all night long and then all the next day. When we finally came up for air, we went to the casino next door. We stayed up drinking all night long and into the early morning. When we finally got hungry, we went to a Denny's down the road with his friend. I'll never forget walking home in the wee hours of the morning, holding hands and feeling totally elated. We ran into Hector Jr., who was living with Hector at the time.

Hector and I stood out on the balcony of his condo. Hector was behind me and told me I was his fantasy. Ever since he was a scrappy kid growing up in Spanish Harlem, he dreamed of having a beautiful white woman as his own. I remember that I was wearing a long skirt with a slit up the side and a matching halter top. Hector was kissing the back of my arms and neck. He untied my halter and ran his hands over my chest while kissing me all over. He slid my skirt off and bent me over the railing, and we made love right there in the open air.

Hector was an amazing lover, powerful and full of passion. I would be turned on just looking at him. He was all muscle. Had an exceptional body. I couldn't get enough.

The next day, we got up and went to work out with Hector Jr. I met Junior's wife and child. I loved how respectful and kind Hector was to them. He had a beautiful family. His trainer at the time was Leandry, who also took care of Hector's son.

We rented a jeep that day, and I put it in my name. Hector didn't even have a license to drive. We drove to this beautiful place a couple of miles long. He took me to a fancy hotel for lunch the following day. From our seats, we had a wonderful view of the entire ocean. It was expansive, similar to how I felt in those days with Hector.

Hector received a call from his wife. She had been tipped off that Hector had brought an American woman to Puerto Rico. She was quite upset. Hector's demeanor changed after that. He was like a scolded child. That whole night, he was very quiet and down. The following day, I decided that it was definitely time to go home.

Hector drove me to the airport, and he promised that he'd turn the jeep in that day. I walked to the gate, and I didn't look back. I was too scared to see whether or not he'd still be standing there. Something had changed. I got on the plane and went home, stifling tears. I didn't know what the future would hold.

It took Hector ten days to return the jeep. I shouldn't have been surprised. It turns out that he let one of his friends drive it. This was when I still trusted Hector with these things. Later, when he asked to put his phone bill under my name, I had become wiser.

I didn't hear from Hector for a while, and I was beginning to wonder if it was for the best. And yet I missed being with him. He finally did call and said he wanted to fly me down to Orlando for the weekend. He had gotten an apartment. Although I was beginning to have my doubts, I simply couldn't refuse. I flew down to Orlando and stayed with him in his apartment. The first night, we lay in his bed and just talked all night long. We talked about everything—his wife, my ex-husband, how my ex had abused me.

It was that night that I told Hector that if he ever hit me, that was the end of it. He could do whatever he pleased, but if he laid a hand on me, there would be no looking back. Hector was listening intently. I was relieved that I said it. Talk turned into silence, and we made love on and off from there.

Not to say too much, but I must admit that Hector had a way of making me feel beautiful. That night, Hector told me to call him Papi! I thought it was amusing at the time, and I obliged, because no one had ever made me feel the way that Hector made me feel that night. The sex was so intense. Hector had a way of making me feel like the most beautiful, sexy woman in the world. I didn't have the courage to tell him that he was my fantasy as well.

Hector Jr. was training with Leandry at that time in Denver. Hector flew me out there as well. I was starting to get used to answering the phone and hearing Hector say where I was going to go next. I was basically self-employed at that point, so I welcomed the travel. On the trip to Denver, I became very domestic. I fixed things; I baked cakes and cookies for all of them.

We went for a ride one day and stopped in a bad part of town. Hector got out at a gas station and was talking to a couple of guys who followed us back to the condo. He said they were fans.

He had to explain again how famous he was, and I just laughed. Hector and I hadn't been out much together in public, so it was still amusing to me when he told me he was famous. I decided to lounge by the pool, and Hector went for a ride with the guys. I found out later he was off to pick up some cocaine. These disappearances were becoming more frequent.

Hector somehow managed to hide his cocaine problem from me for a long time. When he came down to the pool later that day, he didn't recognize me. I had my hair pulled back in a sleek ponytail, wearing a gold bikini and matching sarong and even gold high heels! I was getting stares from the men who were with him. I walked by Hector and dipped into the pool. After swimming around a little, I got out and went over to Hector to give him a kiss. He just stared at me and then started laughing. Recognition overtook him, and he also noticed that the other men were ogling.

Hector dragged me to the hot tub behind the pool. We sat in the warmth for a few minutes, and then he picked me up. He was so strong that he could do this at will. Hector sat me on the edge of the hot tub. To say that the result was steamy and intense would be redundant. I knew that the others were aware of what we were doing, but I felt no shame.

Later, we ventured to a bar in Downtown Denver. I can't even remember how it happened, but Hector and I got into a heated fight. When we finally got home, I called a cab and said I was going to the airport. Hector was in shock. He threatened to break the cab driver's legs if I went. I managed to break away and again flew home in tears. The pattern was becoming quite intense.

Our next encounter would be Las Vegas. Hector was training for a fight. At that same time in 1999, there was the famous fight between Oscar De La Hoya and Felix Trinidad. When he picked me up at the airport, we went straight to the training camp.

It was a typical setup. Hector and I had a lot of sex, and it was getting loud. We'd lay in bed naked, and I'd sit on him backward, giving him a mani-pedi. We were supposed to go to a Warner Bros. party together that night, but Hector said he didn't feel well. He sent a bodyguard to go with me. When I got home, he was asleep.

To make up for it, Hector took me to this fancy restaurant in one of the casinos, and he slipped away for ten minutes. This time it wasn't for drugs. Hector went to a store and bought me a ring. He said it wasn't an engagement ring or anything like that, so I shouldn't get too excited. He just said he felt like buying me something nice. I put the ring on my finger, and I'll never forget the way that it glittered. No one had ever bought me something like that before.

It was the day of the big fight, and we hopped in the limo to go to the weigh-in. Hector warned me one more time that he was really famous, and I gave him my customary laugh in response. Sure, he was probably a big deal. But the fight that I saw wasn't such a big deal, and the only time we ever spent time together was when he was in training. It was confusing, really. Hector told me that he didn't like being famous, that he didn't like the money and never wanted it. He just loved being in that ring. He loved boxing.

But his behavior often said otherwise.

When we finally stepped out of the limo, Hector grabbed my hand and told me that no matter what happens to not let go of him. "Okay, baby," I said with a humorous smile. There was something charming about it. That was when the first flashes went off, and I noticed a crowd of people. Maybe he wasn't kidding after all!

We managed to get through the door and down the steps toward the weigh-in. I noticed whispers and people turning their heads and pointing. That was when the ambush happened.

Tens of thousands of people started running for him. Hector just walked on casually. I had my hand on his shoulder, and we were separated in no time. Security had to grab Hector and pull him inside the secure area. Hector turned around and told security to come get me. They rushed at me and pulled me from the crowd. When I was reunited with Hector, he had a huge smile on his face.

"I told you I was really famous," he said with a boyish grin. For the first time since our relationship began, I felt a chill run down my spine, and I became frightened. I wasn't sure why.

*Oh my god, he is really famous,* I thought to myself. Instead of going to see the other fight, we went back to camp, cleaned up, and went to the hotel to party. Once there, a Spanish woman approached Hector, and he disappeared. Apparently, he had told Jerry to keep an eye on me while he was gone. I didn't even see him go. I called him, I asked Jerry, and all I got was a shrug in response.

I waited for a half hour and finally excused myself to go to the bathroom. But I lied. I went to the limo and told the driver to take me back to the ranch and wait for me while I packed my bags. I was furious and had every right to be. It was the worst thing Hector had ever done to me.

I had turned off my phone and had no desire to speak to him, perhaps ever again. While all this was going on, I was getting hit on by the limo driver on the way to the ranch! I just couldn't escape these guys. He told me I was way too beautiful to be with a bum like Hector. He said he was more than just a limo driver, and he'd worship me if I chose someone like him instead.

Once at the ranch, I packed quickly, but not fast enough. Hector walked into the bedroom.

"What do you think you're doing?" he asked.

"You got the wrong woman if you think I am going to sit here and let you disrespect me!" I yelled at him.

Just then, the limo driver knocked on the door. Hector told the guy that I wasn't going.

"The fuck I'm not!" I hollered, bags in hand. Hector had never seen me that mad before. He fired the limo driver on the spot and actually managed to calm me down. I don't know how he did it. But it was the usual story. He told me he was sorry. He told me he respected that I had left and that I was unwilling to take his shit. He actually seemed impressed.

I stayed that night and unpacked my bags again. We had amazing sex. Of course, it's always great after a big fight, and that was the biggest we'd ever had.

That wouldn't be the last trip to Vegas. It would be the first of many. I flew back about a month later, and we stayed at Bally's. Hector and I got all dressed up to go out for dinner then to a lounge where he would sing and dance for the crowd. He had a big, childish grin on his face while he did it. Once the partying was done, we went back to our room. I was exhausted, but Hector was just getting started. I went to bed, and he went out.

Amazing that I trusted him at all back then. He stayed out all night and all the next day. When he got back to the hotel, he wasn't recognizable. He'd probably been on cocaine the whole time. I asked him where he had been, and he said he was partying with Chavez.

"Doesn't he have a fight tonight?" I asked, thinking it insane that he should party so hard.

"Don't worry about it," Hector replied. He reasoned that Chavez was a trained athlete and shouldn't have any problems fighting. Hector fell asleep and didn't get up till the next day.

I stayed beside him, ordering room service and lying low. Turns out Chavez lost the fight that night. Big surprise.

I flew back to Detroit, Hector flew back to Orlando, and the saga continued.

The next destination was Washington. DC. Hector had been asked to participate in Fight Night for Children. He made sure that they flew me out to join him. He was waiting at the airport when I got off the plane. It was becoming one of my favorite rituals—seeing Macho there, a smile on his face. He was wearing this pair of overalls and a yellow shirt. He looked like a little kid on a farm! I had to laugh. He really did take my breath away. Every time that I saw him, my heart would drop to my stomach.

They gave us a room at the Hilton with free room service, whatever we wanted. I was in heaven. He had been given firm instructions to not have sex the night before a fight, but it wasn't long before we kicked everyone out and went to bed.

The day of the event, Hector couldn't make weight.

"Shirl and I will go run six miles," he said. All the guys looked at me and started to laugh. Apparently, I didn't look like the running type. Little did they know that I would run four miles every day for thirty years. I could probably have outrun them all. So I took Hector up on the challenge. It was amazing running through the streets of DC with Hector. We talked and laughed the whole time and even held hands. Hector was able to sweat it out and made his second weigh-in.

The fight was totally unforgettable. We walked from the dressing room to the waiting room, and it was like everyone was there. High officials, pro athletes, everybody who was anybody.

I was seated in the front row. Hector walked into the ring, and he searched the crowd for me. He located me and held my gaze for a moment, then he gave a simple nod. I could feel my heart fluttering in my chest.

After the match had concluded and Hector was triumphant, a couple of girls came up to me and began to talk. They obviously didn't know that I was there with Hector.

"Isn't he so beautiful?" one of them said.

"Yeah, he's going home with me tonight," another replied. I rolled my eyes to myself.

Macho could see that I was standing with these girls, and he came over to get me. I didn't see him coming.

"Sorry to disappoint you, girls," I said when Macho was in earshot of us. "But that is my man, and he is coming home with me," I added. I was annoyed with them, of course, and wanted to claim my territory. Just then, I felt Macho grab me by the elbow and pull me away.

I was still fuming.

"What the hell was that about?" I asked, Hector still pulling me away.

"Just some starstruck fans, mama. Don't worry about it," he said, trying to calm me down.

By the time we got to the room, I was starting to feel calmer. I undid Hector's laces and ran him a bath then washed him from head to toe. I was hoping that we could spend the rest of the night together in the room, but one of Hector's entourage had brought him some cocaine, and he wanted to party the night away.

So I did what any boxer's girlfriend would do; I changed my long black velvet gown for a short one, with a little peephole in the front and back to remind Hector why he was going home with me and no one else. I think the trick worked because Hector looked impressed.

It was really late when we got to the bar. They were going to close, but because of Hector, they let us in with his entire entourage. They kept the band playing and locked the doors so no one would come in. We partied hard that night, all night long.

The next day, I was the first to awake, and I started packing. All of a sudden, something didn't feel right, and I turned around to look at Hector in bed. He was just staring at me with this glaze in his eyes. He was sweating.

"What is wrong?" I asked. "Are you all right?" I put my packing down, and my heart started beating fast.

"No, I'm not all right," Hector said, not moving his gaze from mine. "I think I am in love with you."

I froze, and at first, I didn't know what to say.

"If you think you're in love with me and you're sweating like that, then something is wrong," I reasoned with him, still not believing that he said it. Hector got very sad and heavy.

"It's going to break Amy's heart," he said, a tinge of fear in his voice. I knew exactly how he felt; he was so sad because he knew it was going to break Amy's heart that he had fallen in love with me. *Hector, I was afraid too.* But instead of saying any of this, I jumped on the bed and pinned his hands down, kissing him all over.

"You love me. You love me. You really, really love me," I kept repeating with utter elation. Hector flipped me over like I didn't weigh a thing. We were laughing and kissing, exploring each other's bodies. Finally, we made love, and I felt so complete on that morning.

But when it was time for me to fly home, I gave Hector an ultimatum. He was supposed to fly home with me, but I finally had the courage to tell Hector that he wasn't coming with me. He had to go home and figure things out. He needed to decide what he wanted, because I couldn't go on the way we were going. I couldn't have him with one foot in and one foot out. I needed all of him.

"I think I'm in love with you too," I said to him, trying to explain. "It isn't fair to either of us the way this is right now." Hector's face just sank, and I felt on the verge of tears. "If I don't hear from you, I will understand and accept your decision. I want us to keep going. I *really* do. But we can't continue the relationship the way it has been."

It was one of the hardest things that I've ever done in my life. I sent the man that I love home to his wife, and I thought there was a real chance that he wouldn't come back.

And he didn't.

Even as I write this, I still feel those old tears wanting to swell.

But I did see Hector again. And I was the one that caused it. Was I betraying myself? Flirting with disaster? I ask myself these questions all the time.

I was in Orlando that December, on vacation with my three sons. My friend Tina came along and stayed for a few days. We had booked a room at the Sheraton City on International Drive. It had been a month since I heard from Hector. Who am I kidding? I was counting the days.

I didn't call him from Michigan, but something changed once I was in Florida. It all made me think of him. *It's just for fun. No big deal,* I reasoned with myself. It was a beautiful day, the sun was shining, and my mood lifted. I thought there was no harm in it. So I called.

I called and told him that I was in Orlando for a week with my family. It was two days later that he called and said to meet him at this place called the Latin Quarter. I went there that night, and I brought Tina with me.

When I first saw Hector, my jaw dropped. It felt like I hadn't seen him in years. He was dressed in solid black leather, and he looked amazing. I had on a see-through black lace dress where bra and panties were the only lining. I wore the dress for effect, needless to say.

Hector had this funny way of walking sideways with his head tilted when he was checking someone out. He just circled me like I was his prey, and that big smile came to his face.

"That's what I am talking about," Hector said in approval.

That night, we danced a lot. Well, actually, Hector was the one who danced a lot. He was always keen to show off his moves.

We got home late that night, and Hector said that he was going to get himself a room so he could be nearby. Tina and I went up to change, and Hector finally called saying that I should come down to meet him.

When we met in the hallway, I was pretty drunk at that point. That was why it didn't sound any alarms in my head when Hector tried to get into one door, noticed that it was locked, and then tried to get into the room next to it. That door was open, and so we went in. There were some condoms and lube on the dresser, and I asked Hector if it was his.

He just told me to not worry about it.

So that night, we made love fast, and I fell asleep in his arms. Maybe a couple of hours went by before I heard someone trying to get into the room. I tried to wake Hector up.

"Macho, get up. Someone is trying to get in!" I said, shaking him. Hector just looked at me and told me not to worry. They weren't going to be able to get in.

Well, they did get in. The next thing I knew, the door was swung open, and the light was turned on. Two men were standing there, and they started to scream, which prompted me to scream too! Hector didn't bat an eye.

The men ran from the room, and I jumped up to get dressed. Hector just lay back down to go to sleep again. It wasn't long before the phone was ringing and the cops showed up. Hector got up casually and answered the door, naked as the day he was born.

As it turned out, we were in the wrong room. Of course, the cops laughed it off and just asked for Hector's autograph, and the hotel gave us another room.

Funny as it might sound, that was one of the first times where I thought to myself, *You know what, he is a little famous.*

When Tina went back to Michigan, Macho stayed and got an adjoining room. I wouldn't see him much during the day, but I'd secretly sneak into his room at night. I wouldn't stay all night though. I made sure that I was back in my room before the boys woke up.

I'll never forget how, on our last day there, he brought his son MC to meet my boys. He bought them all hamburgers and ice cream from room service, and we sat down to eat.

It was after he took his son home that we had several rounds of lovemaking. Hector said he had to run an errand to buy baby formula, and I took that to mean that I wasn't going to see him again. I could actually see it in his eyes.

Before we left Florida, I left Hector a message on his voice mail. It went something like this:

"It was great seeing you, Macho. I really had a wonderful time. But we can't do this again. Your place is with your family, and you need to stay away from me. It isn't fair to keep seeing you like this. I have feelings for you… I don't want to get hurt."

I promised myself that I wouldn't call him again. A day went by, then a week, and then a month. Then I got a call in the middle of the night. It was Hector. He was in a car on his way to Detroit. He spoke quickly, telling me that he loved me and didn't want to live without me.

"What the hell took you so long to figure it out?" I remember asking, still groggy from sleep.

Hector explained that he had a fight in Puerto Rico, and he had been there training for it. That was explanation enough for me at the time. I was so happy.

He made it to Detroit safely, and we got a room at the Courtyard Marriott on Hubbard Drive. I have trouble describing the elation that I felt then. My man was back, and I was finally happy again. Everything felt right with the world.

The next day, I swung by the house to pick up some cash, and the phone rang. The call was from Florida, so I answered it. It was a woman's voice. She said that she was Hector's wife. She found my number in his phone.

"I know you're ugly and fat," she said to me with a laugh.

I was going to stop it right there. I stood up tall and fought back.

"Actually, Amy, I am beautiful. It's your son that is telling you that I'm ugly so that you will feel better about yourself. If you want to act immature, I will hang up this phone and not talk to you. However," I said, shifting my tone, "if you want to be adults and stop talking shit, I will answer your questions." After all, I knew that she had questions.

Just as I thought, Amy chose the latter. I sat there with the phone up to my ear, listening to how she had made Hector a champ, how he was illiterate and no good, and how he would be shit without her. She went on to tell me that he was also no good in bed, had a "little dick," and he never pleasured her.

I wanted to laugh. It was as though she were describing a totally different man.

I calmly replied that I had no problems in the bedroom department with Hector. It's funny, at the time I thought her behavior made no sense, but in retrospect, as a woman, I get it. Her pride was on the line, and putting Hector down was a way of holding onto her pride.

At this point, we were talking about the man I loved, the man I had walked away from twice.

I said, "Amy, if I go to him right now and tell him I don't love him and I don't want to be with him, do you feel you can make it work with him?"

There was silence on the other end for a moment.

"Fuck that illiterate, small-dick motherfucker!" she finally said.

"Okay, it was nice talking to you. Please don't call me again," I replied and hung the phone up quickly.

I hurried back to the Marriott because I had to talk to Hector. I told him everything, the whole conversation, the ugliness of it. It was like his face was set in stone, and he just sat there. Finally, he said, "Fuck that ungrateful bitch."

I could see how he and Amy had once made a fine pair.

Hector went on to say that he did everything to make her happy. His family hated her, and he said that she tried to destroy his relationship with me and with his mother. He became so adamant that he even threatened me. If I tried to come between him and his mother, I wouldn't win. No one comes before Hector's mother and family.

He was in a rage, and I left him to himself. I went home and slept for two whole days. The emotional weight of it was just too much.

Once things had cooled, Hector made it clear that he really wanted to stay. He rented a furnished apartment at the Fairlane Meadows, two blocks away from my home. I told him he couldn't stay at my house with the kids, so Hector did the best he could. He found a gym in Dearborn on Warren Avenue, and he would run in the morning and then go the gym during the day. I would feed the kids at night and then spend time with Hector. We weren't going out as much. We just wanted to spend time together and alone.

It was around this time that Hector's son was fighting in Miami. He asked if I would attend with him, and I felt so proud. But that was nothing compared to Hector's pride seeing his son fight! He even jumped in the ring with him because he couldn't hide his enthusiasm. Hector Jr. was just a chip off the old block.

That time with Hector, just the two of us, was my sexual revolution. My ex-husband never approved of my being sexy, but Hector couldn't get enough. I felt so free. Our sex life just kept getting better and better as well.

One day we were going to meet my family at Chili's for lunch, but before we went, I did a sexy dance for him. I was wearing a metal bra and panties. I completely undressed Hector and tied him naked to a chair. I put on Kid Rock singing "Feel like Makin' Love," and I climbed up on Hector, rubbing my metal bra all over his face. The whole time I was so into it that I didn't realize that I was cutting up his face! He looked like he was enjoying it though, so I kept going. Bless his heart.

By the time we were out of the house and meeting my family, Hector was bleeding on his face. My family had to ask what the hell had happened to him, and Hector just started laughing.

"Oh, well, you know how your sister is," he said with a boyish grin. He proceeded to tell them he didn't have the heart to stop me because I was enjoying myself so much.

I think adding to our physical chemistry was how much we loved to work out together. We ran in the mornings and enjoyed being with each other while we sweated and exerted ourselves. Even in the early days when Hector didn't have any furniture, I'd go to visit him and just jump out of the car, sometimes forgetting to turn it off! I'd burst into his apartment and find him waiting for me with that smile on his face. I'd hop on top of him, and we'd make love on the floor or his one piece of furniture, the couch. Wherever we could find a spot, we'd make love. Each day I couldn't wait to be with him, and he couldn't wait to be with me.

Our odd little family felt more complete when Hector Jr. came to Detroit and began training there. It was so beautiful to see them together. Hector was always playing aloof, and Junior was always trying to impress his father. It was startling sometimes. They both so loved each other and cared for each other, but they had different needs. Hector wanted his son to ask for help, and Junior wanted Macho to recognize all his hard work and to respect him. He had become a great fighter, and he desperately wanted his father to acknowledge that.

Our sexual freedom was only growing, and one day we decided to make a sex tape. I had never done anything like that before. It was actually quite funny, because I kept making him refilm it! I didn't like the angle; I thought that maybe it could look sexier.

"Come on, mama. Let me just enjoy this!" Macho protested. We laughed so hard that night. It makes me think about all the things I did with Hector, such intimate things, that I would never feel comfortable doing with any other person. Hector just made it all feel so right. He encouraged me to be sexy and to be a woman. And I had never felt more like a woman in all my life.

There were more fun nights at Hockeytown with Tony and Kelly. They both loved Hector. We'd party hard on those weekends, but every weekday, Hector would get up and run six miles. I'd make him a fried egg sandwich, he would take a nap, I'd go to work, and he'd head up to the gym. On weekends, we'd run together on Belle Island. It was a funny little routine, and I cherished it. Sometimes I'd drive the car and follow him while he ran. We were like peas in a pod. His wife called on one of these runs, and I answered. She threatened him, and I asked if something was still going on.

"I'm still here, ain't I?" he asked. And he was right. For the first time, he was really, consistently there.

It was around this time that it was really hitting home that people were obsessed with Hector. There was this Detroit police officer who was fascinated by him. Hector just had this effect on people. The officer asked Hector to come speak at a low-income school, and Hector obliged. I remember him telling the kids how important it was to stay in school. If nothing else, for the sports! One kid raised his hand and asked Hector about drugs.

"I ain't no hypocrite," he told the kid. "I'm not going to tell you not to do them because I do."

To say that the kids were fascinated by this candid response was an understatement. Another kid asked him where he lived, and Hector just started laughing.

"Papa was a rolling stone. Wherever I lay my hat is my home," Hector replied. He was always talking about himself in the third person, which I found charming. And he truly was a rolling stone, which somehow rolled into my lap.

Hector got invited to fight on Thomas Hearns's last fight, and so did Laila Ali, so there were a lot of press conferences and events leading up to Hector's next fight. The ladies loved him. They were always cooing and asking for his autograph and being totally disrespectful to me. It was just the way that ladies are about these things, but I was starting to be able to brush it off. It was a week before the fight, and the promoters were totally messing with Hector about the money. On that particular fight, he was doing for cheap, and I asked him why.

"I would rather be doing something than nothing," he replied rather humbly. "I love boxing, mama."

I'll say this right here: people thought Hector was slow. I know it. It's a stereotype of boxers in general, but Hector got the brunt of it. But what people didn't know was that when they thought they were doing one over on him, he was doing two on you. He was very vengeful, even if it took him years to exact his revenge. Sometimes I think that he took advantage of people's assumptions about him.

One of his methods for getting his way on that fight was to simply say no and fly back to Puerto Rico. He refused to take their calls. Finally, they got desperate and called me. Eventually, they relented and gave him an offer that he was happy with, so he flew back. They needed Hector. He was invited to fight on Thomas Hearns's last fight, and so was Laila Ali, so they had already hyped this fight up.

It was just about this time that I got a terrible call from a lady named Angie in Puerto Rico. She claimed that she was the best friend of Hector's wife and also Hector's lover. She said that it was her turn with him and that I needed to be out of the picture.

"Let me get this straight," I said to her. I was getting good at these types of phone calls. "You are his wife's friend, but his lover. And you're calling me…" There was silence on the other end. These kinds of women would expect me to be weak, and she was not prepared for the brick shithouse that I had become. "Listen, bitch," I went on, "there's a reason that he hasn't acknowledged you. It's not your turn, and you're just a closet fuck. If it was your turn, he'd be with you. But he isn't, is he? He's with me. I'm glad we cleared that up. Don't fucking call me again."

I hung up the phone and immediately asked Hector about it. I asked him how she got my number, and he just shrugged and said that she was a family friend trying to make trouble.

I left it at that. Was Hector lying? I don't know, and at the time, I didn't care. Love makes you do and think funny things.

All of Hector's posse flew in for the fight, including Hector Jr. Looking back on it, I think Junior came to every fight. Pretty amazing to think about. The casino put both Hector and Hector Jr. up at the hotel a couple of days before the fight. Jerry Villarreal flew in to work Hector's corner.

To say that I was becoming a tough broad at this time was an understatement! I brought my youngest son to the fight, and he wanted to step in the ring. The security guards were giving us trouble, and I decided to throw them some heat.

"I am his woman," I said, motioning to Hector's corner. "If I am not happy, he will not be happy. I will see to that. And if you want him to fight tonight, you better let my son and me in that ring."

They let us in, of course. And my son was very happy. That's the funny thing about the boxing world. You gotta be tough all the time, in and out of the ring. And you especially have to be tough if you're a boxer's woman! I wasn't pulling any punches.

My whole family came to that fight. We also invited the manager from Hockeytown, our favorite haunt! There was going to be a huge party at Hockeytown after the fight. I knew what I was going to wear most importantly. I had a red patent leather dress with a cutout for my boobs. They were going to be on display. If you got it, flaunt it, I always say. I also had five-inch red patent leather shoes, which took quite some effort to walk in.

I'll never forget Hector doing his little side strut when he saw me in it, circling me and cocking his head in the way that he always did.

"I know you're mine because no one can handle you but me," Hector said, grabbing my hand. "You're so beautiful," he said tenderly.

Painful heels or no painful heels, I was out on the dance floor that night! I even got a great compliment from a girl who came up to me and told me that I was beautiful.

"He must really love you because I have been trying to get his attention all night," the girl explained. "He hasn't taken his eyes off you."

I appreciated that she said that and that she was so honest. The red patent leather dress did what it was supposed to do that night. Sometimes you gotta let the outfit do the talking. Once the party was over, a few of us went up to Hector's room—Hector Jr., my sisters and I, Tony and Jerry. We were all in his bedroom and locked the door. Even the obsessed police officer was trying to get into that room! But we weren't going to let him in because we were passing around a joint.

The people outside the door were banging and calling into the bedroom. We were getting pretty high pretty fast, and we thought it was funny to talk to the crowd through the door, using an Oriental accent and saying, "You been here too long a time." We seemed to think this was hilarious because we were falling over one another, laughing.

Those kinds of nights always felt like pure gold, and I wanted them to last forever. But somehow, the high could never be sustained.

Hector said that he had to go to New York for a few days. He packed his bags, gave me a kiss, and off he went.

Two weeks went by. Not a couple of days. I tried calling him, and he answered once or twice. He explained that after New York, he went to Puerto Rico. He was being really vague. He was strange and distant, but I didn't question him.

And after a few weeks, he came back to Detroit like nothing had happened. But something did happen. He had met some woman at a party in New York and went down to Puerto Rico with her. I guess she wanted to do business with him. She trained Arturo Gatti.

"Did anything happen with her?" I asked.

"No way!" he replied, trying to reassure me.

I let it go. Didn't ask about it again. This was the price. It was the price of loving Hector and keeping him. And I kept paying and paying. I would have kept paying my whole life.

# CHAPTER 4

Hector met some Puerto Rican guys at a bar in Detroit. They were twins, so Hector called one of them Twinny. For some reason, these guys made me really uncomfortable. They introduced Hector to Gary Ball Jr. (Junior Ball), who was one of the head of the Highwaymen, a notorious gang known for murder, racketeering, drug trafficking, and theft. Something just didn't feel right.

So I shouldn't have been surprised when two days went by without me hearing from Hector. He wasn't answering my phone calls either. This was the first major break in what had been a good, solid ride for Hector and me. It had been just him and me.

Day 3 rolled around, and I decided to drive to the apartment to see if he was there. He was still not answering my calls. I saw that the lights were on in the apartment, so I got out of the car and went upstairs. Hector was sitting on the couch, with Junior Ball from the Highwaymen, the twins, and some other guy whom I didn't recognize. He had this expression that said "No big deal" when I saw him. He had been missing for three days.

"Hey, Shirl," he said.

"Hey, Shirl? Really?" I replied, hands on my hips.

"These are my new friends," he said casually.

"Where have you been, Macho?" I asked.

"None of your business," Hector replied. At this point, I was really fuming.

"Can I see you in the dining room for a few minutes?" I asked, not wanting the company of those guys who gave me a terrible feeling in my stomach.

Hector got up from the couch and walked into the dining room.

"What?" Hector asked.

"What the fuck do you mean by *what*? Where have you been, Macho?" I demanded.

"I been with my new friends. Get the fuck out of here and don't embarrass me!" he said, finally getting pretty threatening.

I was trying to hold back tears, but I couldn't anymore. I started to leave, flustered and confused. I only got halfway down the stairs before I realized that it was my friend Moe's apartment that he was staying in. I became indignant.

I marched back up those stairs and flung the door open.

"Hell no!" I barked at him. "I'm not leaving. Take your new friends, and you get the fuck out of here!"

"I will call the police if you don't leave!" he yelled back.

I just started laughing, the tears no longer running down my cheeks. Hector looked at me like I was crazy, and maybe I was.

"Please do," I replied. "You know what they're going to say. Who pays the rent?"

"I do, Shirl. Now get out."

"You give me cash, and I give it to my friend Moe." I walked over and opened both the front windows. I went into the bedroom and started taking his clothes, gear, and gym bags, and I angrily hurled them out the front windows.

Hector just stood watching me.

"Moe is going to tell the cops that I pay the rent. So get the fuck out of here. You're not going to talk to me like this, and you're not going to treat me like this. I don't give a fuck who you are. You're messing with the wrong woman, motherfucker!"

Didn't I say earlier that I had become tough? I sure was tough. I needed to be.

Hector and his friends relented and started picking up his clothes on the stairs. Of course, Hector was calling me a crazy bitch the whole time.

"Yeah, I am a crazy bitch," I replied in triumph.

When they were outside, picking up his clothes on the lawn, I went down and locked the doors. I also threw the rest of his stuff out the windows. Fifteen minutes passed before they jumped in their cars and sped off. My triumph turned into anguish, and I sat on the couch and wept. I can't remember how long I sat there crying. Eventually, I got up and went into the bedroom. I took our beloved sex tape and ripped it apart, lying on the bed among the spools of film.

The next morning, he called me. He said to meet him at the apartment. There were some things he needed to pick up. I told him I'd meet him as long as he came alone.

He came in and immediately went to the bathroom, then behind the dresser, and under the bed. He had stored cocaine everywhere. I just followed him around the whole apartment while he retrieved his stash.

Finally, he sat down on the bed.

"I'm sorry," he finally said.

"Who the hell are you?" I replied. "Nobody leaves for three days and doesn't call or answer their phone."

"I didn't know it was three days," he explained. He was probably so high on cocaine that that was true.

"Have you slept at all?" I asked.

"Not yet."

We lay down on the bed, and Hector just held me in his arms. I started crying again. It felt so good to be in his arms, even though I was still so angry.

"Please don't leave me. Please don't go," he said. Hector was clearly upset. He hated that I ripped up the sex tape. "Mama, why did you do that?" he said with pain in his voice.

"You can't stay here anymore. It's not your apartment. I can't have those people in here."

"They're good people, mama," Hector said, trying to convince me. "Don't be like that."

"How do you know? You just met them," I said, knowing that my instincts about them were right.

To this, Hector had no reply. He was out of the apartment. He moved to the Riverfront Apartments in Downtown Detroit. And that was when things went from bad to worse. Hector was going to make me pay for embarrassing him. I knew him well enough to see that.

Hector and I were hardly alone anymore. It was always Hector, Tony, Twinny, Junior Ball, Pauly, and me. Everything changed. We'd go downtown every Thursday, doing karaoke (so much damn karaoke that Hector broke the machine), the usual stuff. But it wasn't the same. Not for me.

It was May of 2000, Hector's birthday, and I planned a surprise party at one of our favorite steak houses in Dearborn, Kiernan's. I rented a private room, brought two bottles of Cristal, and invited the whole gang. We all waited in the room drinking champagne and prepared to surprise Macho.

That night, Junior Ball talked about how he was going to drive Macho in on a motorcycle for his next fight. It was the Joe Louis fight in Detroit. Close to home! Junior Ball kept his motorcycle parked in Hector's apartment. At least that was what I was told. Hector and I weren't seeing each other as much as we used to, but I was holding on, still.

The night that the fight rolled around, we were all downstairs waiting when I got a call from Felix, Hector's brother. He asked me if Hector was okay, whether he'd been partying the night before. I told him that, in all honesty, I didn't know.

We were all seated in the front row. Hector was prepping to ride in on the motorcycle. In fact, he might even have been sitting on it when they told him they didn't have enough money to pay him to do the fight. Someone came into the audience and grabbed me, and I was told that we were leaving. Hector was with me when we left the building. Truth be told, I think that he was high as a kite that night, so it was all for the best.

We went back to the apartment, and Hector continued getting even higher. This was a side of Hector that had never been shown to me before. I didn't know this man any longer. It wasn't the man whom I fell in love with.

We went into the bedroom, and Hector brought a bottle of champagne that we had managed to spare from his birthday. While he was opening it, I went into the bathroom and took a shower. I came out dressed in a nylon one-piece. It was a red fishnet, matched with red high heels. This might have seemed like a silly move, but now I know, I was trying to keep Hector and make things like they used to be.

I walked over to him. Hector never took his eyes off me. That intimacy wasn't cheap to me. It was everything. If I could just connect with him again in this way, maybe everything would be okay, maybe my fears would disappear.

He took a drink of champagne and snorted a bit of coke. Hector threw me on the bed. The excitement of it was unbelievable. We lay back in bed, and Hector did more cocaine while I drank more champagne.

*You see, he does still love me,* I thought to myself in triumph.

The next day, he was off to New York, and as always, I had no clue if I was going to see him again. The night before was like a dream, but I had to admit to myself in the sobering hours of the morning that I truly didn't know where we stood.

But with Hector, the two-week rule remained. I got a call from him, and he flew me out just about two weeks later. We were staying with George and his wife. When she and I were having a ladies' night, I got a call. I shouldn't even have been surprised about the nature of this call. It was Lisa, the one Hector had met in New York some time back and taken to Puerto Rico.

"Hector wanted me to call you and tell you he doesn't want you here," I remember Lisa saying.

Now I had just gotten off the plane from Detroit, and I was dropped off at the house. I was a little disoriented.

"Who is this?" I replied into the phone.

"I'm his friend," she said quickly, and then the real litany was to follow. "He doesn't love you and doesn't want you here."

"Then why did he fly me down?" I asked a bit indignantly. I was now a pro at these kinds of calls. She stumbled a bit and sounded like she was searching for a response.

"You need to leave," she finally replied.

I just hung up. I couldn't go through it again. I told Amy what had happened. She looked at me in amazement, but I wanted to explain to her that this was just par for the course in the preceding years with Hector.

When Macho finally came home, I told him about the call. His face completely fell, and he went silent.

"She called you and said that?" he finally asked.

"Yes," I replied.

"Come on," he said, taking me to the car. We were going to drive to her house. He was going to confront her, and he wanted me there for it.

To say that the situation was uncomfortable was an understatement. He asked her why she did that to me. Her face turned bright red from the moment that she saw me.

"Yeah, well. Oh…" She stumbled. "Now that I see you, I can see that you guys don't belong together. She needs to go home!" she screamed. She didn't like that I was attractive.

"Who the hell do you think you are?" I asked in an outburst of emotion. "You met him a month ago, and you're telling me all this!" I turned to Hector. "Do you want me to go home?" I asked by way of proving a point.

"No way," he replied. Lisa's face sank.

I was seriously ready to go home. The trip had been a total disaster. At the airport, I asked Hector if he had slept with her. There was no way that he didn't sleep with her for her to talk that way.

Hector admitted that when they went to Puerto Rico, Lisa went, he didn't sleep with her.

"Do you like her like that?" I asked, wanting to know the truth.

"No way, mama. Look at her! How can I want that from her when I have you?"

"Why then? Why did you get involved with her?"

"We were doing coke, and one thing led to another. She was telling me that she could help me get fights."

That was when I realized what was really going one. Cocaine had brought them together. He could be out of his mind with her and share the feeling. I could never do coke with Hector. It wasn't something that we shared. He asked me to do it a couple of times, and I always said no.

It drove it home for me again: I don't know this man anymore. This isn't the man I fell in love with.

When I got on the plane, I was so miserably confused. What happened to the man I love? He was unrecognizable.

I would soon learn that Hector was being convinced to go to rehab, and of all people, by Lisa! Hector told me over the phone that the only way he would go would be if I went with him to support him. We had a long talk on the phone. He said he was sorry, that he was trying to get help, and he wanted just one weekend with me before going to rehab. He was pleading with me, and I softened. I couldn't refuse him no matter how hard I tried.

I said I would only come on one condition: as long as we didn't stay at Lisa's together. As crazy as it sounds, he and I had actually stayed there a bit when I was in New York. Insanity, I know.

Hector agreed, and I was on a flight to New York. He picked me up at the airport, and we went straight to the hotel. It was the Courtyard. Waiting in the room were a couple of bottles of wine because he knew that that was my drink of choice. Candles were lit. He was making an effort.

It was just the two of us in the room that night. We relaxed for the first time in a while. I drank some wine, and Hector was doing cocaine. I didn't like it, but I figured that maybe it would all be done soon after rehab. We ran a bath and got in together. He sat in the back, and I sat in the front. He kissed the back of my neck tenderly and ran his hands down the front of my chest. He started draining the water from the tub. He turned the faucet on again, allowing the water to run down the front of my body.

I went to bed, and Hector stayed up all night, doing coke. He could never sleep.

On the flight home, I felt hopeful. I looked out the window and imagined that things were about to change, that Hector was going to change.

The next day, I called to see how he was doing in rehab. He never went. Hector explained that he didn't think he needed to go. He told me he was going because he thought it was the only way that I'd see him again.

He flew me out to New York and picked me up at the airport. He insisted that I see his next fight. It was at the Turning Stone Casino in New York, and when we arrived, Hector went downstairs and bought this beautiful gold chain with a heart pendant. He came to the room and was so excited to give it to me. It was adorable, I have to admit.

This guy named Tony showed up. He was friends with Hector's wife, and he was sent to see what I looked like. Tony even asked to take a picture of me. I thought it was strange at the time. Tony would go on to tell Amy that Hector bought me the necklace and that I wasn't ugly after all.

Hector got a phone call from her, telling him not to spend *her* money on me.

"Shit, I'm the one making the money!" he had said.

I didn't know what to expect at the fight, and I was a little nervous. I remember that I was wearing this red dress with a slit up the side and cutouts at the chest. It was a beautiful dress. I walked out to go down to the fight, and Hector did his usual dance, tilting his head ear to ear and circling me. Hector put the necklace on me.

"Now you're ready," he said, examining the necklace and the rest of me.

We walked down to the arena together. He found me a chair in the front row, and then he went to work. Just another day at the office for him! Hector walked through the crowds with no shirt on, smiling and laughing, stopping to talk with his fans. They went crazy. They all loved him. But not as much as I did.

In the back, the guys were taping up his hands. I went with him. We could hear the crowd going wild in the arena.

"What time is it?" the crowd yelled.

"It's Macho time!" people echoed back.

I could see Hector getting in the zone. He was focusing. It was so sexy to see him in his element. It was intense for me.

We stepped into the arena and up toward the ring. "Ain't No Stopping Us Now" was playing, and I felt a rush through me.

I sat in my chair in the front row, and Hector jumped in the ring, circling around it. The crowd was going absolutely crazy. Hector stopped and made eye contact with me. A smile came to his lips, and then he was off.

He won ten rounds. Hector was like a beast but so graceful too.

When it was time to leave the arena victoriously, Hector grabbed my arm, and away we went together. We were followed by the whole entourage.

When we got back to the room, Hector shut the door and went straight to the bathroom with one of his entourage. They stayed in there for about twenty minutes. It was no mystery what was going on. When Hector finally came out, he sat in a big chair and called me over to take off his boots.

There was something ceremonious about it. I unlaced them one at a time, feeling like Hector was my hero for the night. He pulled out some more cocaine. Again, this was shocking. I knew that Hector did coke, but he never really did it in front of me. This was new.

*Okay, he probably needs it to block the pain,* I thought to myself. We all had our vices. Mine was wine. Maybe I just needed to let it go. Maybe I had to finally accept all this.

I went to the bathroom to draw Hector a bath. I wanted everyone to leave so that I could be alone with him, because it seemed like in those days we were always surrounded by people. Hector finally got in the bath, and I came and sat on the floor beside him. I was still in awe of seeing him fight that night. I grabbed a washcloth and started cleaning him. A huge smile came to his face.

"That feels so good, mama. Please don't stop," Hector said.

I kept cleaning him, and when he was done, I dried him with a towel from head to toe. He reached down to take my hand and then led me to the bed. I laid him down and gave him a full-body massage using lotion. We made love all night long. Of course, when we were done, Hector was not able to sleep.

We decided to go out to a nightclub, and Hector told me that he was coming back to Detroit with me. Instead of booking airline tickets like normal people, we decided to drive that very night. Well, Hector and Junior Ball drove, and I slept in the back. It seemed like I was the only one who required sleep.

That time in Detroit with him was like old times again. I was feeling more optimistic about the relationship. But Hector had a fight on the horizon in Ontario, Canada. So it wasn't long before I found myself in some strange company.

Felix, Betsy, Jerry, Macho, and I all took an eight-seater island jumper to Ontario, and Lisa came with us as well. I wasn't happy about that, and I certainly wasn't happy when Junior Ball showed up with a group of hookers. They were his working girls at the time.

I remember the way that Hector checked them out, saying, "Damn, damn, damn, look at that." He was proud of his son.

"Don't disrespect me like that," I told him. I hated to see him admire other women. "I could do the same to you."

"Yeah, right," Hector replied and walked off. I was furious.

This would be the start of a battle for jealousy that never seemed to end.

Walking out of the trailer, I saw six Canadian Mounted Police dressed in their traditional uniforms.

"You guys wanna meet Hector Camacho?" I asked. They wholeheartedly agreed, and little did they know that they had just been set up.

I brought the Mounties to the trailer, and Hector was standing there with his entourage. On that particular day, I was wearing a sexy red dress with a rhinestone collar, and I intended to use it for effect. As Hector talked to the Mounties, I rubbed my hands up and down one of the troopers' chest.

"Damn, damn, damn, don't all of you men look fine," I cooed. Hector's face was contorted with rage. But he couldn't do or say a thing. What was he going to do? Beat up a cop?

Felix burst out laughing.

"She just got you back, Macho," Felix said with glee. I felt victorious.

But my show backfired. That night, Hector refused to talk to me, so I just stayed in the room by myself. I had no idea where he was or what he was doing. I would later learn that he was going to drive home without me. That was the plan. But once in the car, he decided that he didn't have the heart, and so he turned back.

When he finally returned to the room, I decided that it was time to deal with it.

We were arguing and fighting when I said, "Listen, I refuse to sit here and have a battle of wits with someone who is unarmed!"

Hector was still unhappy, but a little smile came to his face. Betsy and Felix were cracking up laughing. They'd probably never seen anyone challenge Hector the way that I did. Betsy and Felix were in love themselves. A great couple, and they could probably see the love underneath Hector's and my feuds.

Hector and I would eventually take a limo home. I wasn't getting back on that eight-seater plane. It scared the shit out of me. We stopped on the way and got a few drinks. Then we lay in the back of the limo naked and made love all the way home.

Once I was back in Detroit, Hector had to go to New York. We were at that point where Lisa had totally relented and promised me that there was nothing between her and Hector. She also assured me that nothing ever happened between them.

With that all cleared up, you would think that Hector and I were on solid ground. But you would be wrong. Sometimes even love isn't enough to keep the ground from shifting underneath you. It was when he sullenly informed me that Amy wanted a divorce that I got really confused. I think that Hector always thought she'd never leave him. He was childish in that way. She had already warned him several times that if he stayed with me, she'd file.

It was here that Lisa was actually a big help. She looked up his Social Security number to see what Amy could do on her end. She was on the computer all night long. What she found was surprising to me. All the money was in several accounts under Hector Jr.'s name. Hector had set up his trust accounts for the boys. He was smart, and he planned ahead. That would be a godsend in the end.

I called to congratulate him, and a girl answered the phone.

"Who is this?" I asked, already knowing things were about to get heated. "Why you answering my boyfriend's phone?" There was silence for a moment.

"Hector is sleeping. So I answered the phone."

"Please have him call me. This is his *girlfriend*," I said with great emphasis.

I hung up the phone instantly and had this sick feeling in the pit of my stomach. I was leaning with my back against the wall and just slid down it, the tears beginning to run. I was devastated, and I was also exhausted from all of it. Being in love had already put me through the ringer, and it was just getting started, it seemed.

It was two days before Hector called me back.

"Who the hell was that girl, and why was she answering your phone?"

Hector explained that he met her at a friend's house. She was helping out, I guess. She was flirting with him when he went into the kitchen, so he gave her some of his leftover dinner. That was all he cared to explain.

"I'm tired," he finally said and hung up the phone. I kept calling him back, wanting and needing to hear the whole story. It was comical in a way. I kept calling; he kept picking up. I'd manage to get in a "Motherfucker" or "What the hell" and "Son of a."

Finally, he said, "Why do you keep calling me?"

"Why do you keep picking up the phone?"

"Oh…" And he hung up again. I didn't know whether to laugh or cry, so I just did both.

Weeks went by before he explained. At that point, I was almost past hearing.

Nothing had happened between him and the girl now known as Daisy. They got high a few times and did not have intercourse.

He couldn't figure out why I was so upset.

I didn't talk to him for a while after that. I was so hurt. I questioned why I wasn't enough for him, why he needed to hop in the sack with other girls, even if he didn't have sex with them. Why did our relationship have to be so fucked up?

And that was when Hector had his overdose. Lisa was the one who called me.

"They just released him from the hospital. He needs you," I remember her saying.

I still felt so much anger in my chest, but I softened and became instantly filled with fear. I flew to New York as soon as I could.

Hector and I got a room at the Grand Hyatt. He looked terrible, disheveled, and tired. And the moment that we stepped into the room, he pulled out some cocaine. That was it. I started screaming at him.

"Relax!" he said. "I know what I did wrong, and I'm not going to do it again," he reassured me.

It turns out that Hector was mixing heroin with cocaine. It was his new friend Daisy who introduced him to the heroin. He never mixed his drugs.

*What the hell have I gotten myself into?* I thought to myself. It was getting too intense. I was so scared, but I loved him so much. We were not physically intimate that weekend. I just couldn't do it. The phone rang, and it was Daisy. She had been in a car accident and needed to talk to Hector. I handed the phone to him.

"I don't know why you're calling me because I don't give a shit," he said coldly.

I flew home as soon as possible. It was a disaster. For the first time in my life, I truly did not want to speak to Hector. I didn't know him anymore. He called and said he was going back to rehab.

"I don't want to lose you, Shirl," he said, his voice pleading. "Please come see me before I go."

"No," I said. Maybe it was the first time I ever refused to see him. "I've heard this all before, Macho. I don't believe you."

Now the last thing that Hector can't stand to hear is the word *no*. He is the most persistent man I have ever met. I got phone calls daily from him. Each call became more desperate, more childlike and pleading. Finally, I had had enough. Hector won that round.

I flew to New York, and Macho was waiting for me at the airport. He was always charming when I meet him at the airport. Maybe it was his favorite place, en route to something else. In the fifteen years of knowing him, he was almost always waiting for me there.

I was very anxious on this occasion, but the second I saw him, my heart dropped to my knees. There was the little lost kid, and it was impossible to stay mad at him. I think he knew this. He capitalized on it. If he just waited long enough and time lapsed and I started to miss him, my wall would come crumbling down. It always did.

We had a series of romantic lunches and dinners in the city. I met some of his new friends, and Hector continued to do cocaine. We had fun, and I tried not to think about the drugs. He would be going to the hospital on Monday, and then he was done. Maybe I'd have the old Hector back.

I flew back to Detroit on Sunday, he went to the hospital Monday, and Hector was dismissed on Tuesday. Apparently, he hit some girl in the lunch line. She took a tray to the head. I wish that I could say I was surprised.

Hector drove me out to New York a couple of weeks later. It was the middle of winter. I wouldn't have come, but Macho said that he had a surprise for me. He was trying to make up for his conduct. When he picked me up at the airport, the snow was falling really hard. We got in the car and drove straight up to this bed-and-breakfast in Upstate New York. We almost didn't make it; the roads were so bad. After checking in, we went up to the room. It was so beautiful.

The fireplace was burning, and we got the hot tub rolling. I bounced on the king-size bed like a giddy kid. He told me to get dressed for dinner. I wasn't sure that we'd be able to, because the storm was so bad, but thankfully, the restaurant was only a mile away.

We were the only ones in the place. The owner of the restaurant recognized Hector, so they sat us in front of the big picture window and locked the doors. We watched the snow fall from our table. A complimentary bottle of wine was sent to our table. I'll never forget that Nat King Cole was playing in the background. It would end up being one of the best memories I ever had with Macho.

It was just us two. And whenever it was, things just seemed right. That was the Hector I knew and loved. We talked and watched the snow, ate a sumptuous meal, and chatted with the staff. Hector left a fifty-dollar tip.

When we got back to the room, we lit some candles and opened another bottle of wine. We made love first in the hot tub and then on the bed. Then we drifted off to sleep, at least I did. But in the morning, I noticed Hector had slept as well. Maybe new things were on the horizon?

In the morning, they brought us fresh muffins and orange juice. We stayed at the B and B the whole weekend. It was like a dream.

But reality always kicked in again. Whenever Hector came to Detroit, he stayed with Junior Ball from the Highwaymen. He would still box at Phil's gym, but his cocaine use was back up, especially when around Junior Ball. When we'd go to a restaurant, he'd say that he'd be right back and then go missing for an hour. He'd return with a phone number and a stash of coke. His new hangout became Freer Bar on Michigan Avenue, and he was all set. As long as he had his hangout and his drugs and his gym, Hector was happy.

But Hector still needed to work.

Lisa got him an appearance in Fort Walton. They wanted him to do this fight with a midget. It was a wacky wrestling show. I wasn't happy about this, of course. I flew down to be with him, and Hector said he couldn't wait to see me. We went straight to our room after my arrival, and I was excited to show Macho a new pair of bra and panties that I spend a hundred bucks on. He was in a funny mood. He came up behind me and told me that he knew I liked it rough. He grabbed the front of my bra and just ripped it off.

"Macho, please stop!" I screamed. "That cost too much—"

Before I could plead any more, he ripped off my panties, and I just started crying. He laughed. I was so furious, but his laughter was so infectious that I started laughing too.

The wrestling event had fallen through, and I was happy about that. Lisa got him an appearance doing a grand opening for a new restaurant in Fort Walton. Where once she tried to get rid of me, now she was using me as leverage to try to get Hector to do things. Hector was not happy about the idea, but I really liked it. So Hector agreed.

Hector even agreed to go to my family reunion! By this time, my family really loved Macho. I bought him an outfit that he called "white boys' clothes." He looked so cute! He had on his Tommy Hilfiger shorts and tank top, and he was ready to go. The outfit and Macho were a big hit. He was so funny and entertaining, and people just crowded around him. We played a match of volleyball, and Hector had everyone laughing the whole time. He went after every ball, sweating like a beast. I was beside myself with laughter.

I watched him spend time with my family, and my love for Hector just deepened. He was doing more and more things to make me happy, like going to my nephew's graduation party and the eighteenth birthday of my friend's daughter. He didn't have to do that stuff.

Things were going really well between us when it was time for the restaurant opening. It was October 20, 2000. Hector flew in from New York, and I flew in from Detroit. We took an island hopper to Fort Walton. Our host met us at the airport with a limo and took us to the beautiful hotel.

We had a lovely dinner at the front table, and then Hector signed autographs till ten at night. The next day, there was a fair-like event with water balloons and egg tossing. Hector just had to do the egg toss. I remember smashing an egg on his head, and the crowd went wild. Macho looked at me gravely.

"You're going to pay for that, Shirl," he said.

Well, I did. But it was later, in bed.

Before that, we spent most of that Saturday at the restaurant and finally went back to the hotel. Then I crawled up to him and lay in his arms.

"That wasn't so bad," I whispered in his ear. I thought he was going to exact some kind of sexual torture!

Our next outing was November, when we drove to New York for his son's fight at Madison Square Garden. For my nightclub ensemble after the fight, I had a skintight black patent skirt with matching black patent Marilyn Monroe top and, of course, black heels. Lisa, Hector's new manager, took one look at me and shook her head.

"Ohhhh no," she said. I took this as a compliment. I made sure to put a coat over my dress in order to reveal it at the right time. Hector and George went off to be alone at the bar, and that was when the coat came off.

There were at least four men who came walking over to me that night. I started flirting.

"Which one of you boys wants to buy us a drink?" I asked.

"If you give me a kiss," one of the men replied, "then I will."

I nodded in approval, and the guy went off to get a drink. When he returned, I gave him a kiss on the cheek, and before I removed my lips, Hector came striding over, punched the man, and grabbed my arm. He escorted me out of the bar, leaving George and Lisa. It was all to prove a point after all. And I think that point was clearly made.

We drove back to Detroit that very night, stopping at a hotel and getting a room. Hector was still furious. We had sex, of course, and Hector proceeded to tell me that I was his, and I better get used to that.

"You're mine, Shirl, and I love you so much."

"Baby, all this is yours," I replied, pleased with his admission. "You don't have to make me jealous. I don't want nobody else." It was the truth. It's still the truth. I didn't want anyone else, but I was tired of the way that Hector tried to make me jealous around other women.

I have to admit that I was on autopilot in my life before I met Macho. He made me feel alive. I never wanted to go back to that. It was clear that he was seeing other people, but he assured me that he loved me. Now from my behavior, I know that it wasn't enough. He was spending time with other women, and I could no longer be confident that I was the love of his life. What if he was treating the other women the same way he treated me? What if he had many loves?

He promised me that he never had intercourse with these other women. He did drugs with them and used his sex toys. Half of me always believed him, and the other half didn't. I wanted to believe that he was all mine and that I was all his. The funny thing is that Hector didn't really have a sense that he was doing anything wrong. In his mind, there was no sex, so there was no problem.

As I said, my family loved Macho, and they always knew when he was in town. But that wasn't because I told them. It was because Macho would go through my contacts and call them all on the phone while I was asleep. I tried to stop him from doing this. He was calling important work contacts and asking who they were. So in retaliation, I started going through his phone. It got to the point where when one of Macho's friend saw my number on their phone and it was late, they would call the next morning and ask if Macho was back in town.

These calls happened a lot, since Macho was back in Dearborn training for a fight. Lisa got Macho a fight with pay-per-view. It was called Mucho Macho Madness. Macho brought one of his friends, Sammy, in from New York. The two of them were staying at Junior's one night, and I joined them. We ordered pizza. The delivery guy recognized Hector, so Macho invited him in to stay and party.

The poor delivery guy got so high that he was barking and doing flips on the floor, singing and dancing. Macho kept the guy up for two days, partying. He lost his job after that. Kinda funny that he delivered a pizza and never came back. Macho had this effect on people.

Hector and Sammy stole Junior's limo one night. They did it after Junior fell asleep. They went for a little joyride. Hector drove most of the way then turned the driving over to Sammy. The two of them were low on drugs, so he told Sammy to drive to what was definitely a bad neighborhood. This was no big deal for him. He knew exactly where to find what he wanted and needed. And who was going to mess with Macho?

It turns out the cops pulled them over, and when they rolled the window down, they saw who it was.

"What are you doing here?" one cop asked.

"We're looking for a good restaurant to eat at," Hector replied casually.

"You ain't going to find a good restaurant this late at night. Not in this part of town," the cop replied, a little confused. Hector went into a rage.

"Damn it, Sammy! I told you! Now get me out of here," Hector wailed.

Sammy drove off, shaking his head. He took a lot of crap from Hector. There was this one time they were shopping in a mall in Miami, and Hector grabbed a few pairs of Versace pants and stuffed them in his bag. When it was time to walk out the door, he told Sammy to hold the bag. He took it, and then the alarm went off when he went to leave.

"Run, you fat bastard!" Hector yelled.

"No way, Macho!" Sammy yelled back, and then nerves got the best of him. He took off running to the car. Once he made it, heaving and sweating, Macho pulled a few thousand dollars out of his pocket and showed it to Sammy.

"I have the money," Macho said, laughing. "But I just wanted to see you run."

Sammy was not laughing.

But this happened a lot. Hector liked to steal little things like peanut M&M's, lighters, cheap stuff. Every time we walked out of a store, he'd pull little things out of his pockets and grin like a child. I used to get so mad. I would tell him that one day he'd get arrested. To this, he would just smile.

Hector had been arrested a lot. He wasn't afraid of it.

There was a fight coming up with all three Camachos. Hector, Felix, and Hector Jr. (Mucho Macho Madness) were training down in Florida. I flew in a couple of days before the fight. One day we were walking on the beach, and Macho started with his bullshit whenever a pretty girl passed. He would stop and stare at her till she looked at him. He liked it when I got mad. There were a lot of pretty women in Miami, so you can imagine how many times he tried to hurt me. Even when I explained to him that it was disrespectful and asked him to stop, it just spurred him on.

The morning of the fight, I had had enough. We were staying at a Loews Hotel, one of the nicest in Miami. We were seated at the breakfast table, and Hector and his brother started to argue. I stood up and said that we were in a nice hotel, that they should stop. His brother pushed me, and Hector got up and punched him. A big fight started. His brother was arrested, and Hector and I went back up to the room. It was like conflict followed us wherever we went.

"See? See how much I love you? I hit my brother for you," Macho said in the room.

"I didn't want you to hit your brother. I just didn't want you guys to fight and argue in a nice hotel," I explained.

I was feeling slightly appeased until that afternoon when we went out to lunch in an outdoor café. A pretty girl walked by, and Macho started flirting with her right in front of me. That was it. I lost it. I stood up, picked up a plate, and threw it at his head, walking out of the restaurant.

"Get this crazy bitch out of here," Hector said. I turned around and lunged at him. Pauly from Detroit had to grab me and carry me out of the café.

"I'm okay. Let me down," I said once we were away from the table. He put me down, and I grabbed a bottle of wine and swung it at his head. Pauly dodged it, picked me back up, and walked me all the way back to Loews. Lisa gave me half a Valium to calm me down. Needless to say, I didn't want to go to the fight. I was tired of trying to explain to Hector how much he was hurting me. He thought it was funny.

Macho finally came up and lay down with me on the bed and asked me to go to the fight. He said he was sorry. I wanted to remain strong, but I never could with Macho. It's like he turned me into goo. I went to the fight. Felix got out of jail an hour before it started, and all three Camachos were victorious that night.

After the fight, I started running Hector's bath in the hotel. He spent a few minutes with his entourage and then kicked them all out of the room. Hector sat in a chair, and I sat at his feet, unlacing his boots—our little ritual. I put Hector in the hot bath and washed him, dried him, and then laid him down on the bed. I gave him a full-body massage.

Our next encounter was a weekend in New York, where we got a room in Jersey close to Amy and George. Hector was really depressed, and it scared me. He was rarely depressed on the outside.

He always covered it. As it turned out, his son Ty was in New York and he wanted to see him, but his wife refused to allow it.

He called his sister, who told him to pick Ty up from her place and that they'd keep it a secret. Hector jumped at the chance. He brought me with him, and we picked up the kid, taking him to Toys "R" Us and buying him diapers and toys. We got back to the room, and the three of us lay on the bed. Hector had this huge grin on his face.

"I'm with the two people I love the most," Hector said with a contented smile. Hector and Ty took a nap. Macho tried to have sex with me, but I refused. Sometimes Hector just didn't have a sense of things. He could be simpleminded like that. So instead, we watched TV and stayed in the room that night.

I was the first to wake in the morning, so I went to get some breakfast. When I came back, Hector was taking a bath with his little son. Something inside me just melted at the sight of it. I sat there and watched them for a while, in a daze. To see a baby boy trapped in his father's arms like that. It made me love Hector even more. I didn't want to hurt him ever again. There were so many different sides to the man that I was just in awe. Despite our craziness, my love for him was still growing.

He took Ty back that day, and I flew home, incredibly happy that I was able to see what I had seen, to have been a part of it.

Hector's next gig was at a gentlemen's club in Chicago. Lisa got him the job. He didn't want to do it until he learned that it was right near Detroit, and I could drive down and meet him there.

Hector and I had sex in the bathroom the night we met in Chicago. It may sound funny, but I liked to look at him in the mirror as we made love. He had such an amazing body. He was an athlete after all. Just the sight of him brought me pleasure.

That night, we were to take pictures with the attendees, then have dinner, followed by an awards show. So when I got dressed to go, I wanted to make sure that I got it right. I stepped out of the bathroom wearing a skintight gold crochet dress that made it look like I was nude underneath, and it plunged down in the front, accentuating my cleavage. Hector's first response was delight, but he wasn't so happy later that night when men were trying to take pictures with me.

After dinner, Hector took me upstairs and into the room. He ripped the dress off me and was in a rage.

"You're mine, Shirl. Do you hear me? Mine!" The dress was torn to shreds. I couldn't wear it again.

Lisa was banging on the door, telling Hector that he needed to come back down. She pleaded that they had paid for his time. The fierce and fast lovemaking was done, and I took another shower and found something else to wear.

Perhaps the guests wondered why Macho's girlfriend wore a second dress that night, one that was much more demure.

# CHAPTER 5

It was Easter of 2001 when Hector came to Detroit and stayed at the Courtyard near my house. We took all the boys out to dinner, mine and his. As we sat around the table, I couldn't help but think what a funny little family we made. At the time, his son MC and my son Nikolas were the same age, and they enjoyed playing together.

There was one day where I was watching MC, letting him and Nikolas get into mischief together, when I got a call from Hector. He had to fly to Puerto Rico, and he'd be back in a day or two, he said. This was starting to feel natural to me, to act as a mother to Macho's son. We had a lot of fun too! We went to the drive-in movies in my convertible while MC fell asleep in the back. Nik and MC were like two peas in a pod. But it wasn't long before I felt bad for MC.

Hector's "two days" turned into a week. It broke my heart.

"How could you leave your son with a stranger?" I said, trying to see the situation objectively.

"You're not a stranger, mama. I know you," Hector said with a smile.

"But, Macho, your son doesn't really know me all that well," I reasoned. Although I had to admit, I was starting to feel like I had known the kid since birth.

Hector didn't have much of a reply for this. He packed his bags and took the kid back to New York.

It wasn't long before Hector returned to Detroit by train, this time without his son, and he stayed with Junior Ball. I've already said how much I didn't like Junior Ball when I first met him, and to make matters worse, whenever he and Hector were hanging out, I was told that I wasn't invited. This would make me furious, but my feelings had changed toward Junior Ball over time. I thought he was kind of funny, and you could tell he genuinely liked Hector. When you love someone, you can't help but like the people who love them as well. So I had to let the stuff with Junior slide.

In fact, their relationship was kind of fascinating. These were two seriously strong men, and they genuinely loved each other. It was the way that brothers love each other. It was amazing to see, especially since Junior brought out a whole other side to Hector that I had never seen before.

Not only was there love but Junior Ball also took care of Hector, and he never asked him for anything. Everyone was constantly asking for things from Macho, but not Junior Ball. He was always picking up the bill. Later, I would learn that it wasn't Junior Ball who didn't want me to spend time with the two of them; it was Macho. As it turned out, he was afraid that I'd fall for Junior Ball. Once this came out, I did fall for Junior Ball, in the sense that we became the best of friends. Funny how these things work out.

I was working a job at a new title company, and Macho was doing his usual dance between Florida, New York, and Detroit. Lisa had gotten a fight for Hector and his son in Denver. Macho brought the whole family to Colorado while he trained, and Lisa looked after the kids while he did. I felt like maybe I wasn't needed, so I didn't go. I would later learn that Amy flew in for that fight. It was fine by me. I was focused on my job, focused on myself, and I wasn't going to let anyone take a hammer to my confidence again.

After the fight, Hector immediately came to Detroit and stayed with Junior Ball, of course. Even though the guys hung out a lot, Hector and I still managed to spend a lot of time together. He would come to my son's football games, which he loved. When he was at a playoff game, Macho stood by a fence to be closer to the field. It was then that he was spotted by a sports station that came up to Hector, demanding an interview. That was the last game he went to. In all honesty, I know that he liked the attention, but he wanted those games to be about my son.

Hector was spending so much time with Junior Ball, and it confused me, because Hector was asking me to have his baby.

"I want a little girl. I want to name her Maria, after my mom," Hector confided in me.

If he wanted me to have his baby, then he had a funny way of showing it. He was traveling to Florida a lot, back and forth. On one occasion, when he was leaving for Florida, he started begging me to try and get pregnant. As you know by now, once Hector set his mind on something, there was no stopping him.

Of course, I loved Hector, but there were two things that terrified me. For one, Hector wasn't great with responsibility outside boxing. If I had a young child, he wouldn't be around, and it would be too much to fly back and forth to see him. But the biggest reason I couldn't do it was because of Hector's addiction. Would the drugs have an effect on my baby? Would he take drugs around my baby?

I had to admit, Hector was good with his kids, but they were older then. In fact, he was marvelous with them. He loved to take us all out to dinner, and he was always spending so much money spoiling Nikolas. He let him drive his Jaguar while Hector would fall asleep in the back! Now that's trust.

To try to persuade me further, Hector asked me to come and live with him in Florida. He said that he hated Detroit, that he got into too much trouble there. But I couldn't go to Florida. My life was in Detroit and still is. It's home. My job was going well at the time, and my property turned out to be a wonderful investment. But the biggest reason why I couldn't go was my kids. Hector was a gypsy. I was an independent, capable woman. I wasn't going to rely on something that I shouldn't rely on.

I got a call from Hector when he was down in Florida with Junior Ball and Pauly, who were staying at the Sheraton.

"Please come and see me," he begged over the phone. He told me that he was feeling depressed.

"You are down there with your friends. What's the problem?" I asked. Truly, why would he be depressed when he had his guys by his side?

"You need to get on the next flight out," he said.

I was really concerned. I still wasn't familiar with this other side of Hector at the time. I thought he was always pretty upbeat and full of energy. Maybe he was just trying to win me over. Well, it worked.

I got on the next flight out. Hector met me at the airport. We went to the room, and I noticed that Hector was strangely quiet.

"What's wrong?" I asked, putting down my bag. "Why did you need to see me so bad?" Truth be told, I always promised Hector that if he needed me, I'd be there no matter where he was in the world.

Well, Hector unloaded everything that was on his heavy conscience. Junior Ball and Pauly had stolen a mask from a nearby museum. That was depressing enough, but then Hector admitted that Junior Ball met some girls and that they all made a porno flick together.

That was about all that I needed to hear. I went absolutely crazy, yelling at him and screaming.

"How could you do this to me? How could you do this to *yourself*?" I wailed. "What if this video gets out?"

"I was high at the time, mama. I felt like shit afterward," Hector explained. He also thought that since his face was covered by a mask, no one would recognize him if the video leaked.

"So you cheated on me, and then you called me down here?"

"I didn't cheat on you. I didn't have sex with them. It doesn't matter now," he said, coming close to me. "You're here. You always come when I ask you to," he said with emotion and regret in his voice. "Will you hold me, mama?"

He was like a little repentant boy. I was so mad, but I held him till he fell asleep. I wasn't just mad at Macho; I was furious with all of them.

That next morning, we were going down to their room to have breakfast, and I thought I might give them a piece of my mind. Then one of the girls answered the door.

"Hi, Shelly," the girl had the gall to say.

"You have a lot of nerve to look me in the face and say hello to me after what you did. Making a porno movie with my man!" I said, rage filling me.

The girl came closer, perhaps to explain.

"You better get the fuck out of my face," I added.

The girls were sent home on the next available flight. Someone had to come in there and clean up the mess, and on that occasion, it was me.

I stayed for a few more days with Hector, but the anger still filled me. I couldn't sleep. I just felt sick about it. Hector ended up driving back to Detroit with Junior Ball, and truth be told, I was glad that he made it out of there in one piece.

Actually, things hit a good streak for a while. The mayor of Dearborn found out that Hector was in town and invited him to city hall. Hector called me to tell me the good news. He was so excited. I came down to city hall and found Macho sitting with the mayor. He was wearing one of the handsome suits that I had bought him, and he was smiling with so much dignity and pride. I was filled with happiness at the sight of it. We took pictures with the mayor, and for a moment, Hector and I felt like the most respectable couple in Michigan!

It wasn't a surprise when Hector had to leave town again, this time to Puerto Rico. We decided to have dinner the night before he left. I called him after work because he was supposed to pick me up. But he hadn't shown.

"Where are you?" I asked over the phone.

"I met a new friend, and we're having dinner at the Volcano," he replied. This was a restaurant in Southfield.

"What about our plans?" I asked. He was leaving, and I desperately wanted to spend time with him before he left. "Who is this guy?" I asked.

"Mama, I just met him today, and it's his birthday," he explained. Hector was always making fast friendships, and he could never turn away from them. Needless to say, Hector had left me furious again.

"Fuck him. You just met this guy, Hector. I want to see you!" I protested.

Hector hung up the phone on me. I tried calling him back several times, but he wouldn't pick up.

*He fucked up,* I thought to myself. First, he hung up on me, then he wouldn't answer, and when he finally did, he told me where they were at. It was time for revenge. Within fifteen minutes, I got home and put on the shortest, tightest, lowest-cut black dress that I owned. I drove to the Volcano Bar.

"Oh damn, the men are in trouble tonight," the valet at the bar said.

"No, only one man is in trouble tonight," I replied, straightening my skirt. I walked into the bar feeling confident and set my sights for Hector. I was like the six-million-dollar man *beep beep* till I found my man.

I spotted Macho at the back of the bar. He was with a man who looked like he was straight out of *Boogie Nights*, wearing a fever silk shirt with three buttons opened at the top and a big gold chain around his neck. I walked directly toward him. I will never forget the look on his face! His eyes went wide, and it was like he was saying in slow motion, "Oh shit, here comes Shirl."

"I'm going to the ladies' room. When I come back, you better have a glass of white wine waiting for me," I said with a big grin on my face. I handed him my purse and excused myself. When I returned, he was waiting for me with a big smile and my glass of wine.

His new friend wasn't too happy when Macho and I went onto the dance floor and abandoned him. The guy just stood watching while we partied the night away. And when the evening was done, Macho and I went home together. I guess you can say that my little black dress won.

We lay in bed together that night and laughed our asses off. I just showed up and claimed my guy, and Hector thought it was wonderful. I definitely knew how to take back my man in those days.

Junior Ball was getting into rave parties at this time. He'd use this one building in Detroit. Macho loved to go down there, but I didn't like it at all. My sister and I still went a few times. Laura and Macho were really close. She loved coming along and doing things with the two of us. Macho was always trying to set Laura up with his friends, of course. This would make Laura and I laugh so hard.

There was this time in 2002 where I bought tickets to Cancun for Macho's birthday. He wanted to go to a rave the night before our vacation. I knew this was a bad idea because the plane was leaving at 6:00 a.m., and sure enough, we almost missed our flight. We got into this huge argument in the limo on the way to the airport.

"You party too much!"

"Mama," he said, not wanting to hear it.

"Fuck you. I will go by myself, and you can stay and party all you want," I said, the limo rushing as fast as it could. While I wasn't looking, Hector stole the tickets that sat on the seat and hid them from me. We got to the check-in counter, and I couldn't find them. I was in a panic. Hector pulled out the tickets and taunted me with them.

"Promise that you'll be nice and stop fighting with me," he said. He threatened to not give the tickets back.

I was furious, but I relented. I seriously wanted that vacation, and I didn't want to be angry the whole time. It took everything that I had to be nice to him.

I had to admit to myself then that it wasn't just about stolen plane tickets. Hector was always stealing from me. It was a huge problem that he had since he was a kid. Whenever he left me, I would always check his suitcase to see what he took. There were pictures of us, jewelry, clothes; whatever he wanted, he took. And as I explained before, when we were out together, he was always stealing candy bars, ice cream, little things.

"You're going to go to jail for a candy bar," I said a number of times.

"No one is going to arrest me, Shirl. I'm the Macho Man," he said. Sadly, he was right.

"No one ever bought me gifts and took me on vacation before," he said lovingly on the plane. He was so used to doing things for other people that it felt good to spoil him like that. I liked spending money on my man.

When we checked into the hotel, the staff immediately recognized Hector and upgraded our room. They even sent us a bottle of champagne. It was an all-inclusive resort, and a few strange things happened while we were there.

The owner of the resort had a daughter who lived on the grounds, and she started to follow us around. In fact, she followed us for the whole four days that we were there. Of course, Hector liked this, but it was seriously freaking me out. I would stop and turn around wherever we were walking, and she'd always be there. It was like *Fatal Attraction* or something.

Hector would just laugh it off.

"Leave her alone. She's just starstruck," he said.

Two days into the trip, Hector ran out of cocaine, so we had to take a trip downtown. Hector rolled down the window and asked the locals where he could buy a supply. First, there would be several pictures and autographs. They dropped me off at a bar, and two hours later, Hector came back with a smile on his face. He was happy again.

Our room was amazing and had a Jacuzzi on the balcony, facing the water. Our last night, we got in the Jacuzzi naked, ordered wine from room service, and Macho got high while I sipped my wine. It was wonderful. We slow danced naked on the balcony. Hector didn't care if anyone saw. He was a free spirit like that. We made love in the hot tub under the moonlight, with the sound of the sea as our background music. It was amazing having him to myself. All the time that we had spent apart didn't matter in that moment. The long distance between us just vanished. Whenever Macho and I got together, there was magic between us. It was as though we were one, inseparable. We were in tune with each other—soul mates.

New Year's Eve rolled around, and we went to Andiamo with the Highwaymen. They paid for everything. The Highwaymen knew how to take care of Hector. We would get up onstage and try to salsa dance with each other. Hector knew how, and he was trying to teach me. I tried my best, but I didn't have the rhythm that Hector naturally had. During our entire relationship, I'd never stop trying.

We had a lovely dinner, then I went home, and Hector went to Junior Ball's. He wanted me to go with him, but I was exhausted.

Hector came to my house the next morning, and he didn't look so hot. He went straight to the bathroom and started throwing up. I took him upstairs, and I laid a blanket on the floor, putting a pan next to his head. I tried to cool him off with a cold compress.

"I love you so much, Shirl," Hector said almost inaudibly. "Thanks for taking care of me."

"It's okay," I said, feeling his forehead.

"I am glad you didn't come. You wouldn't have liked what you saw," Hector said. "And I don't like you seeing me like this."

"That's why I didn't go," I replied. "You know I'll always take care of you."

I lay down on the floor beside him and held him in my arms till he fell asleep.

We were spending a lot of time with the Highwaymen in those days. We went to Greek Town for dinner, and Hector excused himself to go outside for a smoke. When he came back, he had this funny look on his face.

"Mama, hurry up. Come outside with me right now," he said. Hector grabbed my hand and pulled me outside before I had time to ask what was going on.

When we got outside, I could see that there was a light rain falling. There were these three men singing the old Temptations song "Just My Imagination," and Hector took me into his arms and started dancing with me in the middle of the street. People and cars stopped and watched as we danced. When the song was over, Macho bent me over and kissed me. The crowd started cheering.

Hector had his romantic moments. He would send me roses at work, or he'd have flowers when I got off a plane. People continue to be fascinated by our relationship. They would ask me a lot why I stay with him knowing that he cheats, steals, and does drugs. There was a lot that Hector did wrong. But it was in moments like the one that night, dancing in the street in the rain, that made me want to stay with him forever.

I reasoned with myself then that I was not in a position to tell him what to do. I wasn't his wife; I wasn't his fiancée. I was faithful to him, yes. But that was totally my choice. I didn't have to be.

Hector had another fight coming up in Florida, so he went down to train. I went to join him, and that was when the phone calls started. Hector wouldn't answer, but I knew better. I finally picked up his phone.

"Look, I'm here visiting my boyfriend, and I would appreciate it if you would stop calling just for the weekend till I'm gone," I said into the phone.

I wasn't too worried about it. These girls had about a two-month life span with him. They would eventually lose their jobs or boyfriends, and then Hector did not want to take care of them, or he didn't want to share his cocaine with them anymore. There was this one time where he had to send a girl home because she was twitching and blinking her eyes, her head bobbing up and down. It freaked him out. When this kind of thing happened, he'd laugh at them and never see them again. These ladies were just for getting high.

"I'm not a whore, Shirl," he'd say to me. And I believed him. But sometimes it would all be too much for me.

"I can't do this anymore, Macho," I said once. "I love you, and this hurts too much."

"I love you, Shirl, and I am giving you more than I gave any other woman. Why can't you be more confident?" he would say.

The sad thing was that he *was* giving me more than he'd given any other woman. And my love was undying, but I was getting tired of the travel and the drugs. I was so exhausted after that weekend that I flew home and stopped taking his calls. I needed a break, and I had to clear my head, which was going crazy with thoughts.

A few weeks passed, and Hector told me he was flying to Detroit. He asked me to pick him up at the airport. When I arrived, Hector wanted to get a room immediately. There was no waiting. I obliged, and we went to the closest hotel by the airport. I told him about this one-piece fishnet stocking that I bought, and I knew that he wanted to see it, so I had it in my bag. I went to the bathroom to put it on, and when I came back, Hector had lit a candle that he bought at the airport.

Hector started pouring the wax from the candle onto my leg. It was poor planning because it wasn't a normal candle but a gel candle. It burned a hole straight through the fishnet and nearly burned a hole in my leg! We had to rip the stocking off, which we were going to do anyway, but I have to say that I still have that burn on my leg.

At the time, I was crying and lay down on the bed. Today I can laugh about it.

I remember how Hector knelt down beside the bed.

"That's not the way that I wanted that to go," Hector said penitently. "This was supposed to be a special night."

"What the hell are you talking about?" I asked, holding a cool towel over the burn. Hector started rubbing his hand up and down my body.

"Shirl, I love you so much, and I have never been with a woman like you," he said. "You are just so beautiful and smart, and I don't know how I got so lucky that you love someone like me," he added, emotion in his eyes.

"Macho, what are you talking about?" I said, not knowing why he was being so sentimental.

"Shirl, will you get engaged to me?" he asked. It was like everything went still. I sat up, feeling my heart pound.

"Are you serious, Macho? Do you realize what you're saying?"

"Yes. I love you very much, and I don't want to lose you."

Despite my happiness, I was still no fool.

"Oh, hell no, you are not getting off that easy. You need to get down on one knee and ask me again!"

"No, mama," Hector said, fighting back.

"Oh, hell yeah you will!" I fought even harder.

And so I made the Macho Man get down on one knee and ask properly. After he did, I jumped on him and knocked him down to the ground.

"You love me!" I said with utter joy. It reminded me of how I felt that very first time he told me that he loved me.

Hector had the biggest smile on his face.

"Yeah, I do," he replied.

We lay in bed the whole night, holding each other.

"Macho, you know what this means? You have to stop seeing other girls. Your idea of being engaged and *my* idea of being engaged may be different. We gotta be on the same page," I explained. "You understand this, right?" I asked, looking deep into his eyes.

"Yes, mama. I do," Hector replied seriously.

The next day, we went to Junior Ball's. I couldn't wait to tell him the good news. I went on a little trip to pick out an engagement ring. I chose the most beautiful one I could find, and then Macho paid for it. That was it. We were engaged. It's hard to explain how happy I was.

Macho had moved some stuff into my house. He totally took over my garage and put a karaoke machine in there, along with some other things. Still, he had to return to Florida for his next fight.

When I came to join him, it was extremely cold in Fort Lauderdale. I remember sitting in the front row at the fight, and Macho did that thing that had become a part of our ritual. He found me in the crowd and made eye contact before he could start the fight.

During the fight, this girl caught my eye. She was sitting outside the ropes and yelling and rooting for Macho, jumping up and down. Something seemed off to me. To be honest, I wanted her to shut up and sit down. But I had to wonder who she was. When the fight was over, she was standing with a crowd of people, and you could tell she was waiting for Hector.

No sooner did I join him than she run up to us as we were walking out and asked if she could give Hector a kiss. So I did what any tough-loving fiancée would do: I pushed her face away and told her to fuck off.

It was later, when we got in the car, that I asked Hector.

"Who the fuck was that?"

"Just a fan, mama," he replied in a relaxed manner.

"Macho, we just got engaged, and already this shit is happening."

"Stop this. You're being crazy," he said, exhausted from his fight.

I didn't want to be that suspicious, doubting woman. But now that I was no longer just the girlfriend but the fiancée, I wasn't going to back down anymore.

We made it back to the hotel and proceeded with our other little ritual. Hector let one of his entourage in, I ran him a hot bath, he did cocaine, I unlaced his boots, he sent everyone out, then I washed him, dried him, and lay down next to him. The ritual was complete.

We ordered room service and a couple of bottles of wine.

Hector and I drove to New York to visit his family. We stayed at the Grand Hyatt, which had become our usual place. The first person we visited was his sister Raquel, and the whole family was there, even Hector's father. I had only met his father one time, and I had tried hard to get his mother and father to take a picture together, but his mother refused. She had a rough history with Macho's father.

The next night, we were hanging out with George, and for some reason, the guys needed to stop at a strip bar. Probably for drugs. Macho and I went up to the VIP room while George stayed downstairs. While we had the VIP room, I thought I would give Hector a private dance. Might as well since I was wearing a black leather halter dress with a slit up the front and matching black stilettos.

I sat Macho down, turned around, leaned over, and rubbed against him. Then I turned around and unfastened my halter and let it drop.

Our timing was perfect because it was just then that George came in. I had to rush to get my top on and jump off Macho! Needless to say, I think that George knew what had just happened. He just laughed and shook his head, saying, "I can't leave you guys alone for two minutes."

Lisa got Hector a fight in North Carolina. When I attended, Macho was in rare form. His drug use just steadily got worse and worse. He was high out of his mind. I begged him to stop getting high before a fight. He assured me that the fight was easy and that I shouldn't worry. Hector always watched the training tapes before a match, and he assumed that his opponent wasn't such a threat.

"Hector is not in any condition to fight," I said to Lisa, pleading. "You need to stop it."

"Don't worry about it. Everything is going to be okay," she assured me. But I was not happy at all.

Hector approached the table where Lisa and I sat, and he was looking really down and melancholy. He sat across from me, and his eyes bored into mine.

"Shirl, did you cheat on me?" he said.

I was speechless. Where was this coming from? But he was deadly serious.

"Hell no, Macho," I said tenderly, leaning into the table. Lisa's eyes went wide. "Baby, you got five different personalities. I don't need to cheat on you. I got a different man every week," I said.

Hector managed a little smile. I still don't know who was telling him such lies. People were always jealous of Macho and me and what we shared. They were always people telling him I was no good for him. I could never understand it. But Hector would not let any of that go too far. He would stop people when they tried to talk shit to him. He'd tell them that they didn't know me and that I'm the woman who loves him.

"I love you, Macho. And I don't want anyone else but you," I said to him at the table. He seemed to believe me because his face lit up again. He was ready to fight.

I took my place in the front row, and things got started after Hector and I made eye contact. But things turned ugly from the start. I kept encouraging him from where I sat, but it was no use. He looked awful. He was off his game. I yelled at him, hoping that my words could give him strength, but it wasn't enough. Hector took a serious beating and lost that fight. It was so painful to watch.

We went back up to the room immediately, and I ran him his bath. He was taking a lot of cocaine, trying to stifle the pain. I sat down beside him and started crying.

"I asked you not to fight like this, Macho," I said, the gruesome images of that match still haunting me.

Hector just smiled. "Don't worry, mama. I'm okay. You gotta take it with a grain of salt," he said like it was no big deal at all. Hector was the one who took the beating, but I was the one who was losing my shit!

I ordered our two bottles of wine and washed Hector down. We lit a whole dozen candles, turned on some soft music, and lay on the bed.

Funny enough, Lisa called our room to make sure everything was okay. She could hear us down the hall. When she came into our room the next morning, she was not so pleased that she had to remove dry wax from everything. I didn't care that she was upset. It was a marvelous night.

# CHAPTER 6

We drove back to Detroit and celebrated both our birthdays. Hector brought me roses at work, and I remember all the women telling me how cute he was. What I didn't tell them was that Macho would sometimes sit outside my job and follow me home, making sure I was not going anywhere else. He had a friend named Rudy who would sit with him and wait.

There was this day at work where my friend Mike, who was helping Benny Napoleon get elected for Wayne County sheriff, was bringing the candidate around to all the offices to meet everyone. Benny, of course, had to ask me how I knew Hector, and I told him that Macho was my fiancée. Benny thought that Hector should come to his benefit party.

"Do you think you can bring him?" Mike asked me.

"Sure, under one condition. If you send me all your mortgage business," I replied.

Mike started laughing. "Sure," he said. Of course, he thought I was joking, but I was actually being serious, savvy businesswoman that I was. The benefit ended up being wonderful, and a good time was had by all. And by the end of it, I approached Mike to let him know that I was not joking. I wanted his business.

Hector went to New York to pick up his mom and brought her back to Detroit. I'll never forget taking her out to dinner in Dearborn and laughing and dancing the night away. Hector would sleep downstairs with his beloved mom while I slept upstairs. He wanted to be sure that she was comfortable. His mom would even hang out with my mom. They played bingo together. Maria gave my mother a chain when she left town, and my mother still has it to this day. It was remarkable how close Hector was with his mom. They'd spend a couple of months out of the year with each other. She would worry about him all the time. But she confided in me that she never worried when he was with me.

Hector and I used to love this bar in Dearborn called Bamboozles. We'd go all the time with my sisters. Hector liked it because they had karaoke. I was no good at karaoke. In fact, there was this one time where a guy said, "He must really love her because that bitch can't sing, and bless him, he gets up there with her each week."

I wasn't offended. It was the truth. I was terrible, but we still had so much fun together.

Macho was in training again in Florida, and sometimes he'd stay at his ex-wife's house. She was always stealing from him, so I guess it was a family thing with them.

"I'm not in love with her, but I'll always care about her," Macho said to me. I still had a hard time approving. She made his life a living hell. But he just wanted to see his kids, and he had to put up with so much shit to do it. He always talked nice about her on television, but in real life, Amy was no saint. Still, he had her back. That was the kind of guy Macho was.

Hector had this thing about calling me for phone sex when he was on a long drive, which was often. I didn't mind. It didn't matter who was in the room with him and where he was. Macho wouldn't be able to sleep. So for almost fifteen years, Hector would call me two, three, four times a day. He was always persistent. If I was out somewhere, he would wait till I got home. He couldn't sleep until I put him to sleep. It was a full-time job.

As time went on, the jealousy never ended. I'll never forget Sammy calling and saying that he got a new job working for a drug lord named Paco. Hector and I came down to New York, and Sammy and Paco picked us up in a limo. Having a job did wonders for Sammy. He was wearing a handsome blue suit, looking happy.

To celebrate, we went out to the Copacabana. Hector did his usual disappearance for drugs, but things got interesting when Paco took an interest in me. He was wearing this huge homemade cowboy hat, and when he finally got me out on the dance floor, he put the hat on my head. He was a strong guy. In fact, for two whole dances, my feet didn't even touch the ground. He was just swinging me around like a rag doll. Needless to say, Hector didn't like this one bit. He was fuming.

We got into a huge argument, and he grabbed me and demanded to leave. Paco was trying to get my phone number because he wanted to send me my own homemade hat. I told him to just let Sammy know when the hat was ready, because I was afraid to give him my number.

Hector was furious. He couldn't believe that I let Paco put his hat on my head. I fought back and told him that he shouldn't have left me, that he should have stopped Paco. Then I started laughing.

"You don't leave a beautiful woman like me alone!" I said humorously. I couldn't stop laughing, but Hector refused to talk to me the rest of the night. He sat in front of his computer and did cocaine for the rest of the night. I was hoping that he got the real message, that cocaine was coming between us, that whenever he disappeared to score his drugs, he had no control over what happened to me.

Hector and I were traveling frequently then. We'd go to New York almost every weekend. Jimmy's Café in the Bronx was one of our favorites, and we'd dance all night long. I had no rhythm, and his mom and sisters would make fun of me, but I didn't care. If my man wanted to dance, then I'd dance. We'd get a room at the Grand Hyatt. Hector would party all night long, unable to stop, and sometimes I'd just sleep in the back of the car while he did it.

The next day was a visit to Whitey and Jeanette. It was a double date at Paquita's. We got a table at the back of the room, and Hector and Whitey got up to get a drink. As Jeanette and I were facing the door and the bar, in walked this woman wearing a top that was just barely held together by strings. Hector looked at her. I couldn't get mad about it because everyone else in the bar looked too. But then he did his walk and his strut that was for me only, tilting his head to one side and marveling at her.

"Hang on, Jeanette. I'll be right back," I said. Hector didn't even see me coming. I walked up to him and slapped him upside the head. "What the fuck are you still looking for?"

Hector turned around toward me. "Oh, shit!" he cried and walked to the bathroom. I followed him, kicking the door open, and sure enough, he was locked away in there with the owner of Paquita's.

"Get your little pussy ass out of the bathroom and talk to me!" I yelled.

"Take her outside," the owner said to two bouncers who were nearby. I grabbed Macho by the curl as they were dragging me out.

"I am not leaving without my man!" I yelled. The two bouncers were trying to carry me out, and I was still holding onto Macho's curl, pulling him with me.

They finally got me outside, and the owner came out following us.

"Calm down," the guy said, "or the police will come."

"Zip up your zipper and mind your own damn business!" I yelled, still raging. "This is between me and my man. Get your ass back in the bar!" He zipped up his zipper, all right, and threw his hands in the air.

"You're on your own, man," the owner said.

Hector and I got in our car, and we were still arguing like crazy. He got out to come to my side to talk to me. I jumped in the driver's side and locked the door fast, then I started driving off. Hector was chasing me, yelling at me to stop. I made it a few blocks and then slowed the car down to a stop, letting Macho in.

When we got to the room, he still couldn't understand why I was so mad.

"We were out as couples, on a double date with friends," I explained. "I can't take any more of your shit. You always do what you can to make me jealous. I used to be so fucking secure, and the more I stay with you, the crazier my life gets!" I said, on the verge of tears.

I eventually cooled off that night, and the following day, we went back to Paquita's to apologize to the owner.

"I'm sorry, man," Hector said.

"I forgot my meds," I explained. I'd laugh about that later. In fact, both Hector and I would laugh our asses off all the way back to Detroit.

The time finally came when Hector sold his house by the ocean in Puerto Rico. He gave Amy fifty thousand bucks as a settlement.

"Why did you do that?" I asked him.

"It's for the kids, mama," Hector explained. It warmed my heart. Every time he went to Puerto Rico, it was drama and heartbreak, but he kept going for the kids.

"All she does is hurt people, mama," Hector explained to me. "She is ghetto. But she is family to me." It's amazing that he kept being so nice to her, because she didn't see it the same way he did at all. She was entitled. It truly hurt him. He always hoped they'd have each other's backs. He wouldn't get mad when she stole from him. It was like he was trying to make up for a marriage that didn't work all that time.

Hector was back in Florida, training. He drove back and forth a lot, staying at Casa Blanca on the ocean. I would fly down to Florida once or twice a month. I have to admit that the first few times I flew down, it was really great. We'd take long walks, holding hands. Okay, we weren't doing long walks on the beach, but we'd go to the grocery store and get a couple of bottles of wine, and I would make homemade spaghetti. We'd light our candles, and I'd cook while he opened the wine. He would sit at the computer and turn on some nice music. After dinner, we'd dance with one another slowly, reconnecting. We kept to ourselves a lot.

This one time, we were sitting in the lobby waiting to go out, and some girl walked up and started talking to him. He introduced me as his fiancée.

"I didn't know you had a fiancée," she said.

"What does it matter?" I asked defensively. She just stomped off in a huff. Hector and I exchanged a look, and my instincts told me the truth with a glance. They had been partying together. Of course, it was the same explanation: he was not easy, he didn't have intercourse with her, and they just partied. I had heard it all before.

I hate to admit it, but it was as much a part of our ritual as the candles, the baths, and the lovemaking. Jealousy and deceit were built into the fabric of our love.

The ritual continued when I returned to Detroit, only to fly back to Florida a couple of weeks later. I had been working a lot in those days, so I was looking forward to going out and partying. Hector flew me into Fort Lauderdale, and we drove straight to his room in Miami.

"Shell," he said to me on that first night. By this time, he could finally pronounce my name, by the way. "I'm really tired. Go down to the bar, have something to drink, and let me rest. We'll spend the whole day together tomorrow, I promise," he said. It was very unlike him. But mama needed a drink, and so I went.

The next morning, Hector complained of still being tired, but I wanted to go out.

"Go lay in the sun," he said. "Have a few margaritas, and when you come back up, we'll go out."

At this point, I was getting a little frustrated, but I did what he said. I went and lay in the sun, had my drinks, then went back up to the room. When I got up there, he told me to lie down for a bit and then we'd go down to the strip to have dinner. I was beginning to think that something was seriously not right.

Dinnertime rolled around, and I finally had to say something.

"Macho, I have been working hard all week, and I want to go have some fun!"

"Okay, mama," he replied. "Get dressed up really nice. Put something fly on, then we will go to dinner and do some dancing."

I was getting excited then. Maybe he was ready to go out. I got dressed up and put on the same black patent leather skirt with a halter top and high patent leather heels. We went to the valet and got the car. Hector drove straight to Burger King, ordered a Whopper, and asked me if I wanted anything to eat.

"Hell no!" I replied, absolutely furious. "I thought we were going out to dinner and dancing."

"You look too good, and I don't feel like fighting with you or someone else because you look so good," Hector explained. Seemed like the jealousy had worn Macho out.

But I was still livid. We went back to the room and got in a huge fight. I changed out of my black dress and went down to the hotel bar, and Hector went back to sleep. When I came up later that night, he said the very same thing he said before.

"I'll make it up to you tomorrow, mama," he said.

Well, tomorrow came, and he was still tired. *What the fuck is going on?* I thought to myself. It was the same story. He was telling me to go downstairs, sit by the pool, have a few drinks, etc. It was the last time. I did all that he told me to do, and again, he wouldn't get up when I returned. He gave me a couple of hundred dollars and told me to go shopping.

Sure, I spent the money, but when I returned, Hector refused to get up to take me to the airport.

"You think I need you to go to the airport?" I said. "I will find any man and get a ride. I gotta go home. I'm working on Monday," I said to him. I had had enough. So I packed my bags, and the whole time Macho just lay there sleeping. I left the room and went to the valet, telling them to bring his Jaguar around. I threw my bags in and made my way to Fort Lauderdale.

*What the hell happened?* I thought to myself the whole way home. I had never seen Hector like that, and it infuriated and frightened me. Something wasn't right.

Two days went by, and Hector finally called me.

"So, bitch, you found a ride to the airport and made it home, I see," he said to me.

"Yeah, as a matter of fact, I drove your car to the airport. Don't worry, baby. I hooked you up. The car is on the top floor in long-term parking, and the keys are under the mat. They won't charge you an arm and a leg."

"What!" he said, and I promptly hung up on him. Apparently, he didn't know that the car was gone. He must have gone and checked because I got another call half an hour later.

"You crazy bitch!" he said. "You took my car to the airport. How the hell am I supposed to get my car in Fort Lauderdale?"

"The same way you expected me to get to the airport. Take a cab, motherfucker!" I hung up again. I was trying to make a point, and I think that it landed.

Two hours went by, and he called me again, this time repentant.

"Shell, you're so fucking bad, and that's the best one you've done yet. I love you, mama, and I will call you later," he said, truly impressed by my antics.

"I love you too. Bye, baby," I said with a smile on my face. I was victorious in that match.

It was around this time that Hector was trying to talk me into moving to Florida. He also kept pressuring me to have his baby. I told him that I simply would never leave my children in Detroit to move to Florida. That whole time, it was clear that Hector didn't like Detroit, but he spent a lot of time there just to make me happy. And part of me thinks that this is why I tolerated those other women. It was a compromise. My children came first, and Hector came second. If that was the way it was going to be, then I had to accept his faults.

Of course, I didn't like it. I wasn't happy about it, but I understood it, and I knew that in the end, Hector would never leave me. He wasn't going anywhere.

Hector was staying with this family in a beautiful home in Florida. Turned out that family ran a phone sex operation out of a real estate office. Leave it to Macho to always find the wrong people to be with no matter where he was.

Hector started playing around with a married woman. She did nails in one of those fancy salons in Florida. When I found out about her, I just started screaming and yelling.

"Macho, you know damn well you are not going nowhere. You are never going to leave me, so don't go breaking up this poor woman's marriage just to have fun!" I screamed at him. Hector just laughed at me, telling me how much he loved me. He would go on to break it off with the woman, and God knows whether or not her marriage survived. I don't even know why I cared, but I did.

The next fight that Lisa got for Hector was in Hollywood, Florida. At that point, he was renting an apartment that was somewhere between Fort Lauderdale and Miami. I hadn't seen the place yet, so I flew in a couple of days before his flight. All the kids were down there staying with Lisa, and Macho picked me up at the airport. We went directly to get something to eat. I can honestly say that Hector was sober then. It was always his protocol to get sober a couple of weeks before a fight, with a few glaring cases where he wasn't able to do that.

The morning of the fight, we went out to breakfast with Junior Ball and his kids. I wanted to get my nails done, so I had Macho drop me off at a nail salon close to the hotel. Now of all the salons to choose, I went to the one where the married woman worked. To make matters worse, she was the one doing my nails. Really, I didn't know all this until Hector came to pick me up and he started saying hello to everyone in the place. They all gave him knowing glances. He sat beside me and put his arms around me.

I gave Hector this look like, "Are you serious?" And he just nodded, affirming what I feared. This was not a great way to start the day, for sure.

There was this woman named Cheena, who I couldn't stand. She was always hanging all over Hector, and back at the hotel, he told me that he invited her to the fight. I was livid.

"I hate that bitch. Why did you invite her?" I said to Macho, thinking the whole situation was just surreal.

"It's not Cheena you have to worry about," Hector said with a smile. "It's her daughter. She turned into a beautiful young woman, and that's why I invited them."

That was it. I had seriously had enough. How much can one woman take?

"I'm not going to your fucking fight. I'm taking the first flight home," I said, rushing toward the luggage.

I put all my things out on the balcony. Hector didn't see me do it. I fashioned the latch so that it wouldn't lock, then I told Macho that I was leaving and ran out the door. I hid in an alcove as Hector followed me. Then when the coast was clear, I ran back into the room and locked the door behind me. Hector was pounding on the door.

"Fuck off!" I yelled back at him. "I am not letting you in, and I am not going to the fight!"

Hector was incensed and went down to Lisa's room. They called me nonstop, and I finally picked up.

"Shell, he has to get in. He has a fight, and he needs his gear," Lisa pleaded with me.

"Look over the balcony, and you'll find it," I said. Sure enough, I had taken all his fighting gear and threw it over the balcony—his boots, cape, everything that he needed. Hector came back up, pounding on the door, and I still wouldn't let him in.

I casually took a shower, and the phone kept ringing in the background. Hector kept knocking at the door. It was around the time that I was covered in shampoo and soap that I turned around to find Hector standing in the bathroom, his legs spread and his arms akimbo on his hips. He was glaring at me, and finally, he picked me up by my throat with one hand. My legs and arms were flailing in the air.

"You better kill me!" I threatened. "You better kill me!"

"What the hell are you saying?" Hector questioned back.

"You better kill me!" I repeated. Hector didn't get it, but years back, I had told him that if he ever hit me, then he better kill me or knock me out because I wouldn't go down that way again. I refused to be hit ever again by a man. I would rather that he take my life.

Hector put me down. "What are you going to do?" he said, and I remained still. "Nothing. That's what I thought." Hector turned around and started walking away. I jumped out of the shower and kicked him behind his knees. Hector began to drop to the floor.

The match was on, and I was willing to fight till the end. I jumped on his back, wrapped my legs around his waist, and started choking him. Hector slowly dropped to the floor; he was desperately trying to smack me off him. But there was too much soap, so his hands kept slipping off. I got off him and then kicked him in the back.

"That's what I'm going to do, motherfucker!" I said in response to his earlier question. "I told you, don't ever put your hands on me!"

Hector managed to crawl into the living room. He was beginning to relent.

"You're not going to go to my fight, are you?" he asked. I looked at him seriously, but I decided it was time to lighten things up after our monumental battle.

"Of course I'm going. Give me an hour to get ready," I said casually. A huge smile came to Hector's lips.

"Okay, baby, I will wait for you," Hector replied, getting up and dusting himself off.

When I finally came down to the lobby, I was a little late, but Hector was waiting for me there. I was wearing my short black Bebe suit with an open jacket. It was gorgeous, and Hector looked at me and nodded. We left holding hands in the limo.

As usual, I sat in the front row, but I was feeling fidgety that night. Already that day, so much had happened. I decided that I needed a drink before the fight started, so I got up from my seat. I didn't wait for Hector and I to make eye contact; I just went. When I was on my way back from having the drink, I was told that Hector was knocked down.

I ran back to my seat, and finally, Hector found me with his eyes. Things took a major turn, and Hector started pummeling his opponent, knocking him down in the third round. It was a TKO. I guess that's the power of eye contact.

Hector left the ring and grabbed my arm, pulling me from the arena. When we got back to the room, he told me to pack my bags and go stay in his son's room. I told him that I wouldn't budge and that I was leaving in the morning. But Hector repeated that I should go to his son's room and wait for him. So I did.

A couple of hours passed, and Macho finally showed up. I had put the chain on the door in case his son and his friends tried to come in, but Hector thought that meant I was trying to lock myself in there with his son! I swear, it was like he was losing his mind.

"That's why you put the chain on!" he said wildly, checking the closets and the bathroom and then grabbing my bags and leading me to the car. We fought the entire way to the apartment.

"Macho, I can't do this anymore. This is insanity," I said to him through tears.

"You're mine, Shelly. You're not going anywhere," he threatened back. When we got to the apartment, he was barking orders at me. "Run me a bath," he said.

"No, I am done, Macho. It's over!" I cried.

"Take off my boots," he said.

"No, first the married woman at the salon, then the daughter, now accusing me of being with your son!" I said. "I can't do this anymore."

Hector took off his own boots that night and ran himself a bath. He opened up a bottle of wine and lit the candles. I couldn't believe he was going through with the routine. I just sat there crying, watching him do it all for himself.

"Come wash me," he said after getting in the bath.

"No," I said through tears.

"You're going to leave me, aren't you, Shell?" he said, keeping his voice steady.

"Yes," I replied softly. He remained silent for a moment and then persisted.

"Get in this bath with me, and I'll wash *you*," Macho said.

"No, I don't want you touching me anymore. It's over, Macho." The tears wouldn't stop coming, and I felt my whole body shaking. "I am leaving in the morning."

Macho got out of the tub immediately and grabbed me, ripping my clothes off me violently.

"You're not going anywhere!" he yelled. "You belong to me. I love you so much! You know how much I love you. I'm not going to lose you," he said, his jaw clenched. He was gripping me tightly.

"It's too late," I said, trying to break free. Hector picked up my clothes, grabbed my suitcase, and left the room, hiding my things from me. Macho literally held me hostage. It lasted for two days, and it was a nightmare.

If I tried to sleep, he would shove cocaine up my nose. He wanted to talk. He *demanded* to talk and to bond as we always did. Hector needed to experience our ritual no matter where we were or what happened between us.

On every other occasion, I would relent. I'd forgive him, and we'd spend the night together as we always did. But not that night. On that night, I simply couldn't do it anymore.

It had been two days. Macho had me wrapped up in a sheet, and he told Junior Ball from Detroit and his kids to watch me while he took a shower. But Junior Ball and the kids were lax in their duties, and as soon as Hector was gone, I ran to the closet and grabbed my things, fleeing.

I ran like my life depended on it to the hotel that was right next door and got myself a room. I remember locking the door behind me and lying on the bed, falling asleep almost immediately. I had never been so exhausted in all my life. For a moment, I felt relief, but I had not escaped.

I went downstairs to grab some food, and wouldn't you have guessed, Hector, Junior Ball, and the boys were in the bar. Hector spotted me and ran toward me.

"I knew you were here," he said. "I had Junior Ball call and check, but he couldn't find your name." I didn't register at the hotel in my real name. I used the name Michelle, but somehow, Hector still knew that I was there. "I'm sorry, Shell. Can we talk?" Hector said, trying to be all sweet.

Just then, my phone rang. I pulled it out to look at it. I had the exact same phone as Junior Ball, so Hector thought that it was Junior Ball's phone. I'm not sure what he was thinking, but he went to grab the phone from my hands and managed to hit me instead. That was it.

I ran from the bar and went back to my room.

"What the hell are you doing?" Junior Ball yelled at Macho, grabbing him to restrain him.

"Were you lying to me, huh? Were you lying to me?" Hector said, thinking that Junior Ball had been trying to protect me.

Leave it to Hector to find me no matter what. I thought I was safe in my room when Hector showed up at the door and would not stop knocking till I let him in.

"I'm sorry," he pleaded. "I didn't mean to hit you, Shell. Can we please talk?"

I decided to let him in, not to forgive him but to tell him that I was leaving and I would never see him again. Funny as it may sound, I just wanted to spend one more night in his arms. So that was exactly what I did. Hector held me the whole night and begged me not to leave him. I was being nice to him then, telling him what he wanted to hear, because I knew that it was the last time.

Once morning came, I was getting on that flight and not looking back. And that was exactly what I did.

I was serious that time. I changed my number and never called him. It was one of the hardest things I had ever done in my life. I still loved him, of course, but the relationship was just so unhealthy that I needed to do what was best for myself.

Jump ahead to 2004, when I was still working at American Premier Title, and the receptionist was sick that day. I was sitting at the front desk, answering the phone. Just then, Twinny walked in.

"Macho needs to talk to you," he said, being the dutiful soldier for Hector. He was sent to get my phone number.

"You got the same number as you used to?" I asked him.

"Yeah," he replied.

"I'll give you a call then," I replied, wanting to get him out of there as quickly as possible.

I hadn't seen Hector since December, and we hadn't spoken either. It was the longest time we had gone without speaking. In the past, I'd give in after a couple of weeks, but I held strong that time, at least I thought.

It was when Twinny told me how much Hector needed to see me that I felt myself soften. He wanted me to come down to Mississippi, as he was down there training for a fight in July. Curiosity got the best of me, and I missed him, so I went.

Hector had brought one of the Las Vegas boys he used to train with. They were staying in this little house together.

"I missed you so much," he said to me with that old sparkle in his eye.

"I missed you too," I said. Hector wanted to be with me and me alone, so we rented a room for a couple of days to catch up on things.

"It was getting too crazy, Macho," I said. "I don't like the insecure person that I've become."

We wandered along the beach, stopping in these little bars, drinking and playing pool. One of the last days that we were together, we stopped and got some Patrón tequila and went back to our room. We both stripped down and took a shower together. We lay on the bed, and Macho took his cocaine out and started drinking the Patrón. I was drinking the tequila as well, and it wasn't long before Hector was taking ice out of the bucket and rolling it all over my body. It was hot in the room, and my skin was warm, so the ice melted quickly.

Macho took a shot of Patrón and spilled it onto my body, licking it off me. It felt so good, the mixture of hot and cold. I came quickly and felt that rush of pleasure that Hector always made me feel.

"Don't you miss this, Shell?" he asked. "I can't do this with anyone but you. I miss this part of our relationship." I had to admit that I missed it as well. He just made me feel so damn good, and I felt myself giving in to him again.

I screwed my head on straight when we got back to the house, and I saw these pictures of him and this girl. He planned on returning to Detroit with me, but after seeing those pictures, all the old memories came rushing back.

"Just stay here," I said to him. "I don't want you coming back to Detroit with me." I ripped up all the pictures of him with that girl and started crying. I was so pissed at myself for giving him a try again. I left, and he stayed and won his fight.

Hector stayed in Mississippi even though there was a warrant out for his arrest. He had broken into a computer store in Mississippi to retrieve his laptop that was getting fixed. Hector was high on cocaine and tequila at the time. At first, the store owner was not going to press charges, but then the shop tried extorting five thousand dollars from Hector. When he said "Fuck you," that was when they pressed charges.

# CHAPTER 7

In January of 2005, he was arrested at Imperial Palace. They found ecstasy in his room. I was sure it wasn't his. He never mixed his drugs. It must have been his little friend's. The room wasn't even in his name, so the charges were later dropped. Unfortunately, it was all over the news. I didn't call him when it all went down. I was still so mad at him. Hector made bail right around the time that a hurricane was striking Mississippi, so he made a break to New York.

Lisa got him another fight in Denver in 2005. At the time, Hector was calling me a lot. He wanted me to come. I told him I was too busy. It wasn't a lie either. My company was going to shut down for a month as one of the girls had done something illegal. My boss told me not to worry, but it was hard not to when I was told that he was changing his name. I sold my house and moved to my income property. I literally started fixing and painting things on my own to save money. I redid the floors and the bathrooms and painted all the walls.

So yeah, I was busy.

On the very last day that I was in my old house, boxes packed up and ready to go, my son came in and said that Hector was at the end of the block with his music blaring. He was just watching the house. I was shocked. I hadn't called or heard from him since the situation with the girl in Mississippi.

I decided to call his number and get to the bottom of things.

"Are you at the end of my street?" I asked, anger in my voice.

"Yes," he said, the music still playing loud.

I sighed and tried to clear my head.

"Come to the house," I said wearily. There was no point of leaving him out there on the street.

It was awkward, to say the least. Things were tense. He saw that the house was turned inside out, so he suggested that we get a room.

Of course he did.

"What are you doing here?" I asked.

"My fight is over, and I'm on my way to New York," he said casually.

Keeping me away from him after he showed up at my doorstep was like keeping a moth from a flame. I couldn't resist. We ended up getting a room and spending the night in each other's arms. We just stayed up the whole night, talking and making love. He dropped me back off at my house in the morning. As the car was pulling away, Hector rolled down the window.

"I love you, Shell," he said.

"I love you too, Macho," I said tenderly. "Goodbye."

He drove off, and I had to wonder what happened to my resolve. What was this madness that we shared? I walked back into the house and decided to take my mind off it. There was too much else that I had to do. The following night, I got a call from him from New York. Apparently, he was with some girl he met in Arizona, Debbie. He left her at Junior's house on the night that we spent together.

You know, I had to laugh. I couldn't think about it. It was beyond absurd.

"Take care of yourself, Macho," I said over the phone.

"Goodbye, Shell," he said, tenderness in his voice. That was it. It was time to get my life back together. I sold my house and moved, and I was determined to start over again.

Two months later, our company opened again. I took a huge loss. It cost over eight grand to sell my house. The market was dropping, and the values were going down. I wasn't going to worry about that either. We were back in business, and I rented out the two upstairs units of my new home. I was going to make it work.

Apparently, Macho returned to Arizona. I knew this because I got several phone calls from this Debbie, asking if I still loved Hector.

"Yes, I will always love him," I would say. "I am just going through something in my life, and I can't deal with the drama that goes with Hector." I went on to explain that we were not together because *I* chose not to be with him, not because *he* did. "Please quit calling me," I finally said.

That didn't stop the calls from coming. She would call all the time.

"You must really be insecure if you keep calling me like this, Debbie," I said the next time. "I am not interested in your life. If Hector needs me, I will always be there for him whether you're with him or not. I chose not to be in a relationship. Just accept that."

None of this was enough, and one of the last calls was to tell me that she was pregnant with Hector's twins, and I burst out laughing.

"What's so funny?" Debbie asked.

"Good luck with that," I said. "He can't take care of himself, let alone twins." Debbie just hung up on me, and I changed my phone number.

Bonita Money came into Hector's life, promising that they would do a reality show together. Hector told me that Bonita threatened Debbie, and that was the end of the relationship. But I tried to put all this out of my mind. I was rebuilding my life and rebuilding my business. It felt good. I didn't need the drama.

I also heard that Hector and Bonita got arrested one night at Paquita's. We still weren't speaking to each other. Months went by, and I ran into Junior in Bamboozles. Junior had kept in touch with Macho, and he gave me his number. I didn't call right away, and when I finally did, Macho was hiding in Bonita's closet.

"This bitch is crazy!" he said to me. "Please buy me a ticket to fly back to Florida," he pleaded.

It seriously sounded like an emergency, so I checked prices. When I called him back, he never answered. Someone told me that Hector got away from Bonita, but not soon enough. She stole $125,000 from his account. Hector found out when he went to the neighbors to call his bank. They said they just wired money from his account to a different account. Hector lost his shit, and the lady at the bank hung up on him. It was all over the news.

Hector landed in jail in May of 2007 on a burglary charge. He was denied bail because he had posted the last time and went missing for two years. He signed his black Crossfire over to his lawyer to pay for the legal fees.

This case was all over the news as well. I was writing Hector in jail, encouraging him to use that time to make a new start of things, use it to stay away from drugs and get sober. I'd send him pictures of his family and pictures of the two of us taken over the years. I also sent him my new phone number and told him that if he needed money or help, he could call me.

It was in September of 2007 that I got a call from Hector. They were going to release him from jail.

"I'm so happy you wrote me, Shell," he said over the phone, his voice sounding clearer. "No one else wrote me, except fans. I'm getting out in a couple of weeks, and I'll call you the day I get out," he said.

"Okay, Macho," I replied, feeling hopeful.

Hector was released from jail on October 7. I flew down that same day to Mississippi, and we got a room at the Hard Rock Hotel. This was the first time I met Scott. He was a prominent businessman in Biloxi, and he had a lot of connections. Scott took care of Hector while he was in Mississippi.

That first night together, we lay in each other's arms just like we used to.

"I'm so sorry for everything, Shell," he said to me tenderly. "Everything I did to you. I'm a changed man. I want your respect again because I've learned my lesson."

I was blushing with happiness. It was everything that I always wanted to hear. I had waited years for him to say those things. It turned out I was the only one who wrote to him in jail, including all his family and friends. They let him make one phone call a couple of weeks before he got out, and he chose to call me.

And I gotta say it, whenever Hector needed to pleasure himself, he said that he thought of me. A lady can't help but be flattered.

The jail stories were unforgettable. He used to take his spinach leaves and dry them out, then he'd roll them in Bible papers and smoke them. He sold these smokes to fellow inmates. They would believe they were drugs and buy them from him. They'd purchase anything from the Macho Man. But the whole time, Hector missed his family.

"What happened to your little Asian friend?" I asked, lifting my brow. Hector just started laughing, and then he pretended like he was crying, mimicking her, probably after he dumped her.

"She said, 'I thought we were going to be a family,'" he said, still laughing. "I said, 'Bitch, I can't even take care of my own family. I don't want one with you!'"

I wasn't surprised by this. Hector could be so cold to women. These girls would get excited about Macho and leave their husbands, kids, and jobs just to be with him, and they'd be around for maybe a month, sometimes two. Hector hated how these women would drop everything.

So was all this a thing of the past? Hector promised that he'd be faithful to me and stay off drugs. He also expressed how much he missed me deeply and truly.

Macho and I were back on. We were going to give it a shot. I was feeling hopeful.

Scott, Hector, and I went to dinner the following night at Ruth's Chris Steak House, located right inside the Hard Rock. Macho couldn't leave the hotel because he was not supposed to be there at all! It was due to the gambling, which he couldn't be around, as he was still on probation. Wasn't a problem for us because we really enjoyed the hotel.

The following morning, Macho came up with a small white bikini that he had bought for me. I put it on, and we spent the day by the swimming pool, lounging and laughing, enjoying each other's company.

We were making love two or three times a day at that point. I finally went home the following day, and Scott and Hector drove me to the airport. I returned to my life, thinking that maybe things had finally come full circle, in a good way.

Hector was invited to Fight Night for Children again in DC that November. He and Scott flew in from Mississippi, and my sister Laura and I flew in from Michigan. George and Sammy drove up from New York. We all stayed at the Hilton and had a great time the first night. We had dinner with all the VIPs and famous boxers at the event: Jake Lamotta, Ernie Shavers, Gerry Cooney, Aaron Pryor, Buster Douglas, Ray Mancini, Michael Spinks, and Roberto Duran. That was only part of the list. Oh, and Joe Frazier fell in love with my sister. We were having the time of our lives, and Macho was totally drug-free that night. Ted Nugent did an amazing rendition of the "Star-Spangled Banner" on his guitar that night.

The following night was the main event. A reporter was interviewing Macho, and he grabbed the microphone and came up to me.

"You're a beautiful young lady. What's your name?" he said.

"You know my name. You'll be screaming it out loud later," I said coyly, and everyone burst into laughter. It was a night I'll never forget. Hector was on the straight and narrow, and we were in love again.

After DC, we rented a car and went to New York to see a fight at Madison Square Garden. Of course, we had to have dinner at Paquita's. I'll never forget when the owner of the restaurant took one look at me and ran out of the restaurant. In my defense, I lot of shit went down in that place.

Macho paid the bill that night, and the rest of the gang decided to hit the town. I was tired, so I went home and slept. But a premonition came to me in the middle of the night: Macho was doing cocaine again. I could just feel it.

I was furious when he came home and my suspicions were founded.

"Just this once, mama," he said. "I have been good for so long."

"Macho, you can't just do it once," I said to him, and he brushed it off. But I knew that trouble lay ahead.

I flew back to Detroit the next day with my sister, and Hector stayed behind to party.

It was around that time that I started flying back and forth to Mississippi a lot. Sometimes I'd stay with Scott, and sometimes I'd get a room with Macho.

The distraction of Mississippi was a good thing because my professional life was plummeting. I had been there for eight years, and out of the blue, my boss came in and said he was leaving the country. Just like that, I was out of job. They also didn't tell me that for the past three months, they hadn't been paying off my company expenses, which were in my name. It all made sense because the mortgage industry took a huge nosedive at the same time. So it also made sense that I couldn't find another job.

I worked hard to rebuild my business during the day while waitressing at night. I even bartended on Saturday nights at the Arab Nightclub. But all this was not enough; I couldn't catch up. I lost my house.

I didn't tell Macho what was really going on. He had enough of his own problems. He was still on probation. He was down in Tampa, training for his tenth world championship. He was under a lot of pressure, and I didn't want to add any more to it. Besides, "responsibility" wasn't Hector's middle name.

I decided to go back to school. My mom lived in California, and there was a radiology program there that only cost two thousand dollars for a two-year program. My kids were doing fine. They were older then, and two of them were in college, so they got an apartment above their father's bar and worked for him while going to school. I was seriously tired of working three jobs at that point and still not getting anywhere, so I packed everything I could fit in my Explorer and drove with my son Hassan to California.

It didn't matter to Macho where I was. I could just jump on a plane and fly to him. He was wonderful during that time. He would send money once or twice a month while I started the program. I had to do six months of voluntary work in a hospital for radiology before I could start the actual program, so I attended Alvarado Hospital and got the ball rolling on my new career.

I was flying back and forth a lot to see the kids and Macho. Hector had a big fight in Houston, Texas. I flew in on the early morning flight, and Hector picked me up at the airport. As usual, he wasn't supposed to have sex before the fight, but once we were in the room alone.

We took a little nap and met up with Patrick and Gigi, who had come to see Hector's fight. Leo and Angelo Dundee were there too. Sammy and Leandry were in Macho's corner.

Hector got dressed before the fight, and then he walked around the hotel half naked because he was so restless. Once we were all in the back getting ready to go, the entourage pumped Macho up. Leandry screamed, "What time is it?" And everybody screamed back, "Macho time!"

We walked out into the arena, and I took my seat in the front row. Macho made his eye contact and proceeded to deliver a TKO in the seventh round. The crowd went totally crazy. Afterward, he did a few interviews, then we made our way up to the room.

Dressed, coked up, and ready to go, Macho and I came down to find out that Patrick had been arrested. He was trying to get to Hector to congratulate him, and some security guards knocked him down. Hector was furious. Gigi and I went back up to the room, and Hector went to get Patrick out of jail. It took hours. When they finally got back, Hector sent everyone away. We stayed in our room for the rest of the night.

Things were getting more domestic between us. We rented an extended stay-type place in Tampa, Florida. Hector was still on probation; he was still doing drugs, but at least we were bonding. Every morning we would get up and run together. I would ride the bike too while Hector ran. We'd come home, and I'd make him breakfast, then we'd nap.

We loved our healthy routine, and we even added a book into the mix. Truly, there was nothing else to do. I'd make Hector's dinner, and he'd tell me all his life stories. I would give Hector a massage and then rub medicine on his feet. Hector would eventually fall asleep, something he was getting better at, and his stories would play around in my head at night—some of them good and some of them bad.

I had picked up a litter of stray cats, and the kittens became part of our little routine as well. I'd lay by the pool and read. Hector loved that I read so much. This time that we shared was right after the hurricane, so there weren't very many restaurants open. That was fine by me because I loved to cook. If we really felt adventurous, we'd sneak into Alabama and go to the Olive Garden. We loved that restaurant.

It was the first time we were living together, just he and I. We'd walk over to the Sonic every night for ice cream, and there was no one else around. It was like we were the only two people in the world.

One morning Macho and I woke up with flea bites from the cats. I was getting more attached the kittens, so I was afraid that Hector was going to be mad, but not him. In fact, I rarely ever saw Macho get angry in those days. When he really was, he'd walk away and let it pass. The problem was fixed at Walmart with a couple of flea bombs and spray. At that point, there were about twenty cats. They had been abandoned in the storm. Even though I had to buy twenty pounds of cat food, Hector just smiled when he watched me feed them. He was so patient.

One day Hector's son Christian called and was angry with Hector about not spending time with him. I found that Hector truly loved his kids, but he just didn't know how to show it. That being said, he started trust accounts for all his sons, and he paid cash for the house that Amy was living in. He always paid the child support, something that Amy never told the boys. But it was like Macho never stood up for himself against Amy. He let her say what she wanted and never said anything bad about her in return.

Macho had tears in his eyes after that call from Christian, and I went on a tirade in Hector's defense. I always defended him in a way that he could never do for himself.

"Thank you, Shell," he said to me. "I will never forget you staying here with me and sticking up for me with my son. I love you so much."

We embraced, and I felt tears coming to my eyes too.

Hector and I decided to take dance lessons to pass the time. We went driving through the neighborhood to find a teacher and stopped into a studio one day. There was this really nice couple who owned the place. They just loved the idea of giving lessons to Hector

Camacho! But Macho made it clear that the lessons weren't for him; they were for me.

Hector's thirty-day pass came through, and it was time to go back to Detroit to see my kids. We packed everything in the car, and off we went. I made sure there was enough cat food and someone to feed them, but I still cried when we left.

"I always knew you were a beautiful person," Macho said in the car. "But I didn't realize how beautiful till I saw you cry over a bunch of stupid cats."

I was wiping away my tears, but I couldn't tell him I was crying for two reasons. I was crying for the cats, and I was also crying because I didn't want to leave the little domestic life that we had shared together. It was the life where it was just him and me.

Macho made sure that he had enough cocaine before we left. We went to this Latin restaurant the night before, and I sat at the bar while he went to make a purchase. Little did he know, he'd have a close call with the cops that night. Needless to say, he decided to do the drive to Detroit stone-cold sober.

And maybe that was why we got into a big fight, or perhaps we both sensed that things were about to change.

In Detroit, he dropped me off at the house with the boys and went to Junior's to meet his new fiancée, Ashley.

Inevitably, our perfect little bubble of a world was burst. I went to California; Macho went to New York, Orlando, and back to Mississippi. He was trying to get his probation moved to Florida and was eventually successful.

Sammy and I flew to Mississippi to help him make the move. We stayed in a hotel close to his probation zone, and when Macho got the transfer, we packed up his bags and started for Florida by car. Macho wanted to drive by the prison and say goodbye to everybody, take pictures, etc. So we went, and Hector took pictures by the front gate. But that wasn't enough. We had to drive all around the prison while he took a video saying goodbye to the place. You'd think he was saying goodbye to a vacation home or something.

Sammy and I were laughing. It was pretty cute. We got on the expressway to Florida, and Sammy wanted to stop one last time at a restaurant and get some sandwiches, so I got off at the nearest exit. All of a sudden, we were surrounded by ten police vehicles with sirens and bullhorns. Some guy was yelling at us through the bullhorn to pull over and roll our windows up.

Men rushed toward us and told us to get out and put our hands up. We were asked for our licenses and then told to put our hands on top of our heads.

"What are you doing taking videos of prison?" one officer barked. Relief came to me as I realized what this was about.

"This is Hector Camacho," I said. "We are driving him back to Florida because he just had his probation transferred. He was taking pictures because he was saying goodbye to Mississippi and the prison where he stayed," I explained. The officer looked at me intently and then at Hector.

We sat there for ten or fifteen minutes with our hands on our heads while they verified this with his probation officer. Then they made him erase the video.

We were let go after that. We still went to the restaurant and bought our sandwiches and then got back on the freeway and started to drive to Florida. It was about half an hour later that we realized we were safe, and we all just started laughing. The tension was broken.

Thank God they did not search Macho because he had cocaine in his pocket.

Halfway through the drive, we stopped at the Olive Garden to grab something to eat. Sammy and I split a bottle of wine, so Macho thought it best that he drive. Using MapQuest, we still managed to drive in circles in Florida. It kept telling Macho to turn left! Since Sammy and I were drunk, we just kept laughing, but Macho was so mad at both of us.

"You can't talk to each other!" he yelled from the driver's seat. Sammy just kept poking me from behind, and the laughing continued.

Eventually, by the grace of God, we made it to Tampa.

Macho and I got our own room, and Sammy got his own. We bought more wine to allow the party to continue.

Hector started doing cocaine as soon as we were settled in the room, but I was tired and went to sleep. When I got up, I saw Macho at the computer. He was totally naked and just stoned out of his mind. I walked up to him and put my arms around him and just started to cry. The drugs were going to kill him. Hector smiled.

"Don't cry, mama," he said. "I am going to be okay."

I just held him in my arms and kissed the top of his head. I was accustomed to this kind of agony.

We stayed holed up in the room the whole day.

Hector went to Miami the next day in order to do a reality show called *Mira Quién Baila*. I was mad that he was going because he was so near to Amy, but Hector said that he'd stay with MC. He needed to do the show. But Amy started being so mean to him that he just left.

"Why do you keep going back there, Macho?" I asked over the phone.

"I miss the kids, mama," he said to me.

Hector met me at my mom's trailer park in San Diego. It was a park for senior citizens. He stayed with us the whole month of December in 2008. Hector was showered with gifts over Christmas. Mom and my sister got him some great stuff from the Coach store, and he was over the moon.

San Diego was good for Hector because he could go back and forth to Los Angeles. I'm pretty sure it was in LA that he was getting his cocaine. I went with him one time, and we stopped in this barbershop for a few hours. There was also a restaurant he'd go to a lot, because he knew the owner. One time, Hector's fight was on TV, so we all sat down together to watch and have dinner. It was an old fight but thrilling to see him on the small screen.

We went to this fabulous Mexican restaurant with my sister and her family, and the whole place just went wild when Macho walked in. They asked for autographs and gave us free T-shirts. Hector was so cool about these things. When we got home, we were in my room, and his phone started beeping. It was a text message from some girl. I texted her back.

"Who is this?"

"You know me, Hector," she texted.

I called the number, and the girl answered.

"I'm a friend of Hector's," she explained. "Who are you?"

"I am his fiancée," I said icily.

"I didn't know he had one," she replied.

"Why should he have to tell you anything?" I asked. "He clearly doesn't care, because he let me call you back."

"Oh," she replied, unsure what to say.

"What do you do?" I asked.

"I'm a prostitute," she admitted to me. I just started laughing. "What's so funny?" she asked, offended.

"Stay on the line," I said. Just another stupid woman who thought that Hector took her seriously. I felt bad for her actually. I handed Hector the phone.

"Fuck that whore," Hector said. "I don't want to talk to her!"

I think that she could hear that on the line because she hung up. That was it. No more texting from her.

Despite this triumph, Hector and I went to the store to get something to drink, and we started fighting.

"I am sorry, mama. Damn, I was doing so good!" he said.

"Fuck off," I said furiously, letting him off at my mom's and going to my sister's. Apparently, Hector didn't have the key because he broke into the trailer and the cops came. They didn't do anything, of course, once they saw who he was.

We eventually made up, and Hector called me his soul mate and said that he didn't want to live without me.

"I've fallen back in love with you," he said. "You're the only woman for me."

I forgave him. I always did. Till his dying day and beyond.

You'd think that run-in with the cops would deter him, but the next day, Macho was walking around the trailer park naked and smoking a cigarette. I had to laugh. The neighbors had pulled all their shades closed and put up signs to keep out. I couldn't figure out why they didn't want to look. Hector had an amazing physique!

We took my jeep one day and went to stay at the Roosevelt Hotel. Hotels were the safe place for Hector and me. They were the escape. It was a Saturday night, and we planned to stay all day Sunday and lie by the pool. When we got there, we went out to dinner and got a bottle of Patrón afterward.

Hector went to a barbershop in order to get some cocaine.

On the elevator ride up to the room, I recognized a man I knew from New York. We had a little conversation, and Hector remained silent.

Once we had all our supplies, we went up to the room and got in the hot tub. We opened the curtains, and Hector pressed me against the window naked and started licking my neck, making his way down my body.

Hector finally laid me on the bed and the passionate lovemaking began. We fell asleep in each other's arms that night, or so I thought at the time. At six o'clock in the morning, he made me get up and leave. He was really upset, and I couldn't understand why.

There was traffic as we left, so we stopped for breakfast. Hector actually accused me of going to meet that man from the elevator! He was so livid. It took some time, but I finally convinced him that nothing happened. I was furious that he was being so irrational.

It wasn't long before Hector's month pass was up, and it was time to leave California. I'll never forget our last night together, listening to the radio and dancing in each other's arms totally naked, holding on to each other. When we awoke, I took him to the airport. Yet again, I would have to say goodbye to him. I couldn't stop the tears.

"I hate leaving because I never know when I'm going to see you again," he said. "It's hard for me too," he added, pushing away one of my tears. It made me feel better that he said that.

I finally finished my volunteer hospital work, and I was set to start my program in September.

On March 20, 3:00 a.m. California time, I received a call from my eldest son.

"Mama, Baba's dead," he said. *Baba* is Arabic for *father*. "We are at the hospital, and he is gone."

It was like a bad dream. I had to have my son repeat himself three times to let it sink in. I hung up the phone and just started crying. My sister and brother-in-law were leaving on a flight at eight in the morning to pick up my sister Laura.

In California, I sat on the couch in my mother's living room. The first person I called was Macho. He was still asleep, and I was crying so hard he couldn't understand me. I finally said the bad news clearly enough.

"I'm so sorry, mama," he said. "How are the boys doing?"

"I don't know," I said. "I love you, and I'll call you later." That was all that I could really say.

"I love you too," Macho replied.

The second person I called was my sister Dana. She was a saint, getting me a flight first thing that morning, and the next thing I knew, my mom was helping me pack. She told me to take more clothes, but I wouldn't listen. I just threw everything in the case in a daze.

I was on the first plane to Detroit, and it was a bizarre flight. Midway through, we had an emergency stop in Denver. There was a woman on the plane who started attacking some guy. She thought he was touching her.

When I finally got to Detroit, I was exhausted, but I went straight to my in-laws' house. All the kids were there. The whole thing was like a nightmare. There were the assets to deal with, but no one fought over anything. I didn't want my children to inherit my late ex's bar business.

Macho flew in. He was going to be the best man at Junior Ball's wedding, but Macho actually took the groom's car to come and see me. Everyone was calling, looking for Junior's car, and Macho just turned his phone off. We bought a fifth of Patrón and got a room at the Courtyard. For the first time in our relationship, I let Macho take care of me.

"I'm going to buy a house in Tampa," Macho said to me. "And I want you and the kids to come live with me."

It was such an amazing offer, but I couldn't take my kids away from their friends and lives. It was so wonderful that Macho wanted to take care of us.

I flew out one weekend, and we stayed at St. Pete. Macho was sober, and we'd get up in the mornings to walk to the local bagel shop, holding hands and buying groceries. I would run up and down the beach, and sometimes I'd lie by the pool and drink margaritas. We would spend the whole weekend together before I flew home.

Macho had to get back to Tampa to train. He had a big fight in May against Yori Boy Campas. I started working three jobs to help my kids out. I was at a title company again and working at Pucks Bar, which my nephew owned. I also worked at J.S. Fields, which was a place my sister managed. I couldn't help but think how my kids had lost everything—their jobs, their father, and their hearts. I was working to fix it.

I would text Macho his appointments with the probation officer, and I'd inform Linda, his attorney, as well. I wanted to make sure that Macho was staying on track.

I flew into Tampa on March 8, 2009, and Danny, Macho's friend, picked me up at the airport. I couldn't wait to see Hector. The drive from Tampa to Orlando was the longest of my life. The anticipation was building. When we got to the hotel, he was waiting for me outside. I jumped out of the car and gave him a huge hug and kiss. I just fell into his arms.

But Macho didn't look well. We went to dinner with the kids, and when we got back to the room, Hector started having cramps and a fever. I called Junior and Pauly and told them I was taking Hector to the emergency room. We spent the whole night before the fight in the hospital. Macho was hooked up to an IV. They finally let us go around 1:00 a.m. I begged Macho not to fight.

"Don't be silly. I'll be fine," he said.

That day, Ashley, Pauly, and I stayed by the pool drinking. Junior trained and worked with Macho. Hector had told me that his ex would be at the fight, and it was the first time we'd ever met. I was nervous and frustrated.

"I just want to tell you I love you," Macho had said to me for reassurance. "That's why you are here. You're my woman."

When I was getting dressed before the fight, I couldn't zip up my dress, so I went down to the bar where Junior and Pauly were.

That was when his ex walked in. I was not impressed, I must admit. She was loud and tacky and not a nice person. I went back up to the room to tell Macho that she had arrived.

When I went back to the bar, she was still there. I ordered a glass of wine. Amy and Brinette never even made eye contact. I finished my glass and walked out with class.

Before the fight began, Hector made eye contact and then went for it. It was a draw, and I remember jumping into the ring to support my man. There was an interview after the fight, and Hector and I walked hand in hand through the lobby. The ex walked out of the bathroom as we were getting into the elevator, and she came over to start some shit. I could tell instantly.

I wanted to cool things down, so I invited her and her friend up to the room for a drink. Later, Macho would admit that he was done with her and wanted her to go. The only reason that he invited her was so that she could see that there was something real between him and me. He wanted to drive it home to her.

The next day, Macho and I went and stayed at the Hilton Garden. We stopped at a sex store and got a fun outfit and some fruit-flavored gel. We locked ourselves in our hotel room for two days, having sex and enjoying each other. It was magical.

After I flew home, Hector signed a contract with a TV company in Tampa. He was staying with Carlos, one of their employees.

"Why did you sign with them?" I asked.

"I don't have anything else going on, so I might as well," he replied.

I flew down several times while he was there, staying at Carlos's house. It was seriously uncomfortable because he had a girlfriend, and the house was tiny. I would make us all dinner. There was one night we went to a boxing function, and Hector spilled wine down the front of my dress because I looked too good. I was wearing this beautiful low-cut black gown. The jealousy would never cease.

I'll never forget when Macho was going to two schools—traffic school and a different school for probation. I would pick him up, and he would have this huge smile on his face.

"I'm so happy!" he would say. "I realized what was missing the whole time. My whole life, I always did drugs because I didn't know what was missing. I finally realized that I wanted to go back to school. That was what was missing."

"Please come to Detroit with me," I begged. "I will get you a tutor!"

"Maybe," Hector said, considering it. I had never seen him happier than I did that time he was going back to school. It was the happiest he had ever been.

I was still working three jobs, and it was killing me. I really didn't have the time to go see him, so he would fly to Detroit. He wanted to go to Chicago to a Wachovia Bank, where all his accounts were. Detroit didn't have a Wachovia. We took a 6:00 a.m. morning train.

Well, on that 6:00 a.m. train, Hector decided that he wanted to have sex. Should I have been surprised? We snuck into one of the bathrooms and had very *loud* sex in fact. People knew what we were doing. We weren't trying to be subtle.

We took a cab to Wachovia from the train station, and the cab driver waited while Hector went into the bank. Once Hector was done, he asked the cabbie where the largest Latin community was in town, and he drove us there. Like usual, I was dropped off at a bar while Hector disappeared for an hour in search of cocaine. That being done, we had dinner at a local restaurant and then caught the next train home.

Hector stayed with me for a few days after our little adventure to Chicago, but I couldn't see him much because I was working my ass off. This made Macho angry, but I tried to explain to him that I was helping my kids. When I was more stable, I'd be able to spend more time with him.

Hector came into the bar that I was working at on a Saturday night. When I was done, I went with him to Junior Ball's. Macho said that if I stayed out and partied with him, he would come to work with me on Sunday. So I stayed out and partied, but Macho certainly didn't come to work with me on Sunday. Well, that is to say, he came in at 4:00 p.m., ate dinner, then drove back to Tampa. I have to admit that it hurt my feelings. I wanted to go back with him to Florida.

Hector wanted me to leave my kids to go with him. He wanted me to leave my jobs too. There was no chance in hell. I let him go. He was so hurt about it.

"I can see you're working three jobs," he said. "You have to get your life back on track. But I don't understand why you won't come stay with me."

The truth was that there was no security attached to being with Hector. I needed security. I needed something solid. My kids just lost their father. I couldn't leave them.

The one or two times that I did visit Hector in Tampa, it was so hard. Something felt wrong about it.

# CHAPTER 8

In January 2010, Hector was posing for *Playgirl* magazine. I was working for a new company at the time and was in a meeting with my boss. My phone was ringing off the hook the whole time. I finally excused myself from the meeting and answered my phone.

"Mama, I need you to talk dirty to me. I am at a *Playgirl* shoot. They want to take a picture of a unicorn on my dick, and I can't get hard," Hector said.

"Are you kidding me right now, Macho?" I said in disbelief. "I am in a huge meeting, and I cannot talk dirty to you." I hung up the phone and couldn't help but laugh.

Macho and I decided to get tattoos together. I got mine first. I chose a heart with Hector's name on it. He went next. I have to explain that this was done long distance, so I called Macho to tell him that my tattoo was done, and then he called me back to tell me that his was done.

"I did it, Shell!" he said from New York. "I got your tattoo!"

"Did you get my name?" I asked, filled with excitement.

"No, I got a unicorn on my dick!" he said, with equal excitement.

"Are you kidding me?" I said in defeat and disbelief. "You messing with me?"

"No, I really did, mama."

"What the hell does that have to do with *me*?" I asked.

"It means only one person," he explained. "You're the one person!"

I was so mad that I just hung up the phone. It was much later that I would ask how he stayed hard the whole time while they did the unicorn. Apparently, the tattoo artist's wife had something to do with it.

I got a chance to fly down to Tampa in February 2010 because we were going to the Super Bowl. I was so excited. I had not seen Hector in a while, and my job was really draining the life out of me. I needed a break. We spoke on the phone a lot and had phone sex all the time. Still, it wasn't the same.

We stayed at his training camp with two other guys. The first night that I got there, we had to sleep on bunk beds. I was so tired that I didn't even care or even notice the house he was living in.

"Don't go out of the house by yourself," Macho warned me. That should have been the first clue. The next morning, when I woke up, the house was a total mess. There were only men living there, so it was to be expected. I was seriously made uncomfortable by the other guys in the house.

I made an effort to clean the place. I started with the kitchen, where there were roaches everywhere.

"Can we stay in a hotel?" I begged. "I don't feel comfortable here!"

"No way," Hector replied. "This is where I live, and I'm staying."

Hector then told me that we weren't going to the Super Bowl. He did not want to go to Miami because he thought that he would just get into trouble. Hector was still on probation, and that meant no hotel and no Super Bowl. I was not happy about this. Macho was taking steroid shots at the time. They were really expensive and supposed to be "all natural." He had to go to doctors to take them, so he left me alone and went with Eddie to get it done.

There was a Mardi Gras celebration that February in Tampa. Hector's brother Felix invited us to go, and I accepted. I took a shower, and I'll never forget these gigantic spiders along the ceiling of the bathroom and cockroaches on the floor. I was so overwhelmed that I started crying.

"I don't belong here. Can we please get a room?" I said to Macho.

"No. These are my friends, and I am not going to let you talk bad about them," Hector replied.

"I am not talking about them. I have a phobia of bugs, and I can't sleep here," I explained.

Hector refused again, so when Felix arrived to go to Mardi Gras, I got my clothes out of the trunk and dressed. Felix and Betsy just started laughing; they really didn't believe I kept my clothes in the trunk.

Felix and his wife, Betsy, were always keeping tabs on Macho. They were really close. Felix would come and check on Macho as often as possible. Betsy would visit and clean the apartment and make sure he was okay. They were always trying to get Macho to stay with them and get cleaned up.

"I am who I am," Macho would say. He often refused their help.

So we all went down to Mardi Gras. It was so much fun. We stood and watched the parade, and they threw beads at us. I got pretty drunk, but it would help me to go back to the house and sleep with the roaches. Felix and Betsy stayed in a hotel, and I was so jealous.

My drinking got worse the following night when we all went out to a nice dinner. I asked again if Macho and I could get a room, and he got so angry. He made me sleep in the back room by myself. I was terrified. The next morning, I got up and took the car to the beach and fell asleep there. I decided to get a room for myself, but my new debit card was still on order, and there was no bank in Florida where I could replace the card sooner.

Macho wasn't speaking to me at this point.

"Macho, please," I said, lying beside him in the room where he was sleeping on his own. "I don't feel like we're connecting. We always connect. Can we just go get our own space so I can be close to you?"

Macho went completely crazy on me after that. No matter how long we stayed apart, we always managed to connect, but it just wasn't happening. I had never seen Macho that upset in all my life. He started yelling at me, and he pinned me down on the bed. He held my arms down while I screamed and yelled.

This was the first time in our relationship that I was afraid of him. I had to get out of there. I grabbed the keys and left the house. I went down to Chili's and got a drink, my only consolation.

When I returned, Macho was still incensed. He started accusing me of picking up a man when I went to the beach alone. He picked up a chair and started throwing it. Then he picked up other pieces of furniture and did the same.

Eddie came in to rescue me, and I started crying.

"Take me to the airport. I want to go home!" I said to Eddie through my tears. "I've never seen him like this."

Looking back on it, it was the steroids that he was taking. I'm sure of it. He wouldn't frighten me like that again.

"No problem," Macho said in his fury. "Take the bitch back to the airport!"

And so that was what Eddie did. I took my luggage and didn't look back. I called my sister, and she was able to get me a hotel room at the airport, because I couldn't switch my flights. I'll never forget ordering room service and taking a hot bath, finally feeling safe. It was three o'clock in the afternoon. I just got in bed and cried for the rest of the day. He had scared me. For the first time, Macho had truly scared me.

My mother called me the next day. She and Hector were really close, and they talked on the phone all the time. Macho had called her.

"Mom, I almost hurt Shelly, and I love her so much. I will never forgive myself," he told her. "Tell her I love her and I am sorry. Everything is going to be all right."

I had to forgive him again. It was the drugs that caused it. It was always the drugs.

A month later, he went to New York with Sammy, and I got a call. It was Sammy begging me to end the fight with Hector.

"No way," I said. Sammy laughed.

"You will. It's just that not enough time has gone by," he said. Sammy was right. It was because it was still too soon. I returned my focus to my business, and that was that.

Hector was finally in rehearsals for *Mira Quién Baila*. He called and left a message saying that he had finally gotten on a reality show. He always wanted to be in one. I was really happy for him, but it was still too soon to forgive him.

Eddie called in October 2009. He told me that Hector went to Orlando, and his ex called the police on him. Eddie wanted Macho to sign power of attorney over to him so he could get him a lawyer. I knew what to do. I called Linda, who had been Hector's attorney previously. She always took care of Hector. Apparently, while Hector was in jail, his ex came by and stole his car.

"I don't feel sorry for you one bit," I told Hector over the phone. "She always does this to you, and at this point, you deserve it." Since the insurance was in his and her name jointly, there was nothing that he could do about it. The only action he could take would be to sell the car, which he did. She called the police again when he came to retrieve the car, but that time, what Hector had done was totally legal.

Hector wanted me to come visit him in Miami, but I was too busy working. I was still bartending and working my day job at the time. My hope was to help my kids to buy another house. At that point, I was renting an upper unit in Dearborn that was super cheap. It had no furniture, just a bed set. I didn't need anything else. I was working so much that I didn't have time to sit on a couch.

One night I was watching Hector on *Mira Quién Baila*, and I called him.

"What's wrong with you?" I said. "You have more rhythm than that!" I teased. It was nice to hear his voice and to see him on TV, but I was not ready to see him in person.

I finally took a weekend off and flew to Tampa. Eddie and Hector picked me up at the airport. It was the first time that I saw him since the incident. Eddie went off in Macho's car and left us alone. We went straight to the Hyatt at the airport. Macho and I entered the room, removed our clothes, and showered together. I poured both of us a glass of wine, and we lay down on the bed, talking and making love just like we used to. We spent the whole weekend like that.

He asked me again to move to Florida, but I told him it was still not possible. My kids were doing better and getting older. So perhaps with time, it would be possible. We spent the weekend talking about us and where we were going. It was very healing in a way. I caught a plane on Sunday and left Macho at the airport. That was our relationship—a series of departures and arrivals.

Macho's next fight was in Kissimmee, Florida. He called and asked me to come down, but I was still so busy.

"I'll look into taking some time off soon," I told him over the phone. "Good luck with the fight, and we'll talk later," I added. I didn't know that I was going to mention it, but I had to speak up. "My father is not doing well," I said. "They didn't give him long to live." I was unsure that I could handle any more death.

"I'm sorry, Shell," Macho said. "I'll try to come up soon."

Even though I didn't go to that fight, I did hear that Felix kicked Eddie out of it, because he was still trying to obtain Hector's power of attorney. Amazing. People were always trying to get things from Hector. They never realized how smart he really was. If you thought you were pulling the wool over his eyes, it was because he was letting you think that he wasn't smart. You thought you were taking from him? He was taking twice as much from you. That was the game that he played.

I had no free time between visiting my dad in the hospital and working my jobs. I was beyond exhausted. But it helped when Macho came up twice to see my dad—once in the nursing home and once in the hospital. My father eventually went to Chicago for better care, but it wasn't enough. My dad passed away on September 13, 2010. He always loved Macho, who would sit with him for an hour just telling stories. My dad couldn't speak at that point. He could only listen, and I am sure he didn't understand a word Macho was saying, but he was just happy that he was there. I'm still grateful to Macho for that. He didn't have to do it, but he knew it made my dad happy.

Macho was flying back and forth between Puerto Rico and Florida. He was doing really well, and I was so proud of him. I was doing better too, but I had no life. He started doing *El Gordo y la Flaca* when he called to ask me to move to Puerto Rico with him.

"I love you, Shell," he said. "And I want you to move to Puerto Rico. I got a new job, and I can take care of you."

"Soon, baby," I said. "Just have patience."

"Are you faithful to me?" he asked. The truth was that I was very much faithful. There was no time to be unfaithful! Hector brought up jail in Mississippi.

"Don't think I went to jail because you were not around to take care of me," Hector teased.

"You only go to jail when I'm busy, so there must be something to that," I teased back.

In February 2011, Macho was shot at for the first time. He told me he stopped to buy some cocaine, and when he came out of the trailer, that was when two guys approached him with guns. He jumped into the car with the door open and turned on the gas. The car took off, and the driver's side door hit one of the men. It knocked the guy to the ground. Bullets started flying everywhere. Hector wanted to report it, but he went to the wrong precinct. They told him there was nothing they could do, so they let him go. He called me and told me all this, and I just started crying and begging him to come back to Detroit.

"Stop being silly," he said. "I'm safe here. Everybody loves me here. They must not have known who I am, or they wouldn't have tried to shoot me," Hector said.

In March, Macho went to visit the kids. He stayed at his ex's house again, which I hated. While he was sleeping, someone stole $7,000 dollars out of his pocket. The ex started chasing him with a knife, so jokingly, Macho went running through the neighborhood with his hands in the air, screaming.

"Help me! Help me! She is going to kill me!" he wailed. The neighbors called the police. When they arrived to take a report, they told Hector that if he pressed charges, they would arrest both of them. Of course, Macho didn't press charges. When Hector left, Amy called the police back and pressed charges against him.

By April, there was a warrant out for his arrest. After Macho left, Amy called and made a report that he had grabbed his son and stomped on him. Macho would never do such a thing. It ended up going to court, and because of Macho's record, he had no chance. His son testified against him. I think he was set up to do this. Macho tried calling his youngest son to ask him to tell the truth.

"Don't do that, Macho," I reasoned with him. "They live with her." This completely tore Hector up. He finally realized that no matter what he did or how hard he tried, it just wasn't worth the trouble she put him through. It was the first time in his life that he stopped paying child support. He was so devastated that his children testified against him. It was a betrayal.

Macho came to visit me in July even though his new management team tried to stop him. They made up fake interviews, anything to get him to stay. I actually was happy to have Macho stay there. I wasn't giving him my all at the time. I let him go because I knew he and I were making plans for me to move to Puerto Rico in the future. His management was actually doing good things for him, and it was the best choice at the time.

His management played with his head though. They told him that I wasn't waiting for him. They told him I was moving on.

"No way," he argued back. "You don't know my woman." He was right. They didn't. I had already told my kids that as soon as I bought them a house, I was moving to Puerto Rico. Thankfully, Hector kept visiting me.

At the next encounter, we were so eager that at the airport, I was all over him the minute I saw him. I was just kissing and holding him.

"See, this is my woman!" Hector said to people who were staring at us. He was laughing with happiness. "She loves me too much."

As soon as we got in the car, we removed our pants and had sex in the front seat. We couldn't wait to get to my apartment. He looked so good while we were making love that my heart just stopped. He'd never stop having this effect on me.

We went out to dinner at Chili's because Hector liked the salmon there. We stopped and grabbed some wine when we were done and headed back to the apartment. It was very hot out, and he was not happy that there was no air in my apartment. Hector was only supposed to stay for a few days, but he stayed for a week. He wanted to see the boys, so I said that we'd have dinner with them during his stay.

There were a couple of free days before I had to go to work. I took a week off bartending, but not the day job. Macho wanted to go have lunch in Mexicantown, so we went to Armando's on Vernor. As usual, Hector told me to order a margarita and that he'd be right back. Two margaritas and thirty minutes later, he walked back in and paid the bill, taking me to another little corner bar. We sat there for a few minutes, then some man came walking in. Macho met him in the bathroom and came out smiling. I knew what was going on.

Sadly, I had to get up and go to work on Monday. Macho was not happy about it, but that's life. He drove me to work and took my car. When he picked me up at the end of the day, Macho was really high. We went to Fishbone in Detroit. Hector just loved the crab legs. It's funny that I have a photographic memory of all the things Macho liked to eat!

It was still hot, so on the way home, we grabbed a bottle of Patrón. We showered together and then walked around the apartment with no clothes on. We lay in bed drinking while Hector got high. Sadly, our vices helped to connect us.

Around one o'clock in the morning, I told him I had to get some sleep, but he was not ready to stop talking. He kept me up till four in the morning. Hector finally let me drift off to sleep for a couple of hours.

When I woke up, I saw that my phone was in Hector's hand. My clients were texting me at the time, and Hector was questioning me and looking through my phone.

"Do not call those people back. That's business!" I said to him. "Please don't." I managed to get the phone away from him for long enough to take a shower and get ready for work. My phone kept texting me. It was strictly business stuff, but he got out-of-his-mind mad.

"Who is that, Shell?" he said. "You cheating on me?" We started fighting over it.

"Macho, please don't do this!" I said. "I have worked very hard to get my life back on track, and I love you so much. I don't bother you because you have good things going for you, and I am trying not to act crazy anymore," I explained. But Hector wouldn't stop. He even tried to stop me from going to work.

"You're mine, and you're not going anywhere!" Macho said. "I love you so much, Shell. I will kill that motherfucker."

"You have nothing to worry about!" I said, trying to calm him down. "I am so busy working that I don't have time for anything."

We were fighting from the bedroom to the living room, yelling across the way. Hector finally stormed into the living room and wrestled me to the floor and sat on top of me naked, pinning my hands down with his knees. He kept saying the same things.

"I love you. You're mine, and you're not going anywhere!" he said in a fury.

"Listen, Macho. I haven't asked you for help. I have been working my ass off! I promised myself I'd never depend on a man again to take care of me," I said, still trying to talk sense into him. It wasn't working; I had to change tactics. I softened. "Okay, baby. I won't go to work. Give me a kiss."

He did, and then he released me. As soon as he did, I took both my hands and placed them on his ass, scooting out from underneath him. Then I stood up and kicked him sideways.

"Now listen, there is no other man, and I am going to work! I will see you when I get back." I stormed out, but not before seeing that big funny smile on his face.

"I think that's why we're still together," Hector said lovingly. I didn't have time to smile. I grabbed my keys and ran out of the apartment before he could get up.

Hector called me an hour later, laughing his ass off.

"I'm so sorry," he said. "But that's what you do to me. You have fun at work, and I'll see you when you get home. I love you, Shell." That was when I finally had the chance to laugh. I really related to the crazy feelings he was having.

"I love you too, Macho," I said. I took the rest of the week off work. I wanted to spend as much time with him as possible.

On Wednesday, we took the boys out to dinner at Andiamo in Dearborn. Macho was so happy to see the boys, and they were happy to see him too. The dinner was wonderful. We ordered bottles of wine and just sat there for hours, talking. Macho told the boys stories, which had them in tears with laughter.

"I can see why you can't leave right now, Shell," he said in the car on the way home. "I saw pain in the boys' eyes. You're doing the right thing. Your boys need you too much right now. I will wait," he said. I started tearing up instantly.

"Thank you," I said. "It won't be too much longer, I promise." Hector was going to Germany soon, and he asked me to get a passport for Nikolas to go along too.

On Thursday, we took a trip back to Mexicantown. We went straight to the bar, and Macho went for a walk. While I was sitting there, this man approached me. He was wearing a hospital bracelet. He actually tried to pick me up.

"No, thanks," I said. "I'm waiting for my fiancé to meet me here."

"Can I use your phone to call for a ride?" he asked. This made me suspicious.

"Give me the number, and I will call it," I said, not wanting to leave him hanging. He didn't know the number.

"I'll remember if I can dial it," he said, trying again.

"Okay," I replied. I dialed *67 before he used the phone so that I could block my number then handed it to him. He dialed for a minute.

"Aha! I got your number now!" he said. I just started laughing.

"I don't think so. I blocked it," I replied. Macho finally returned while we were laughing, and he immediately got jealous.

"That's what you get when you leave a beautiful woman like me sitting alone in a bar," I said, teasing him. "Are you serious? This guy just got out of a mental ward. Take me out of here," I said, not wanting to argue over it. We went back to my apartment but stopped to get some red wine first.

That was the night that I got Macho onto Facebook. I set up his profile and showed him how to use it himself. I also showed him a web page that proved that Bonita Money stole from Hector's bank account. He called Art and gave him my address so that there was a place to send information. Hector was so excited when he got off the phone. He had been trying to get that information for years.

"How is the book coming?" he asked me.

"I'm still working on it," I said. I had poster boards all over the apartment and tried to finish it in my spare time. Hector really wanted that book—a book and a roast. He was determined. I promise him no matter what I would get it done.

We had this wonderful music night together where we were shooting old song ideas back and forth. We started by playing "I Need You" by Tim McGraw and Faith Hill. We played it five times in a row, dancing in the living room with no clothes, just holding each other and rocking back and forth. He asked me to find this one song called "Street Life," and when I played it, he started crying.

"The first time I was in jail, every time I heard that song, I would start to cry," he explained. We stayed up all night talking. For such a tough guy, Hector Camacho was remarkably sensitive.

"I'm sorry for hurting you at the bar. I love you so much," I said.

"Please let's go get married," Hector said. "Let's do this, Shell. Let's get married."

"I will when I come to Puerto Rico, because right now, I still need time. And I don't want you to see other girls once we get married," I said, turning serious. "But still, I promise that I'll come when I can."

"Promise to come soon," he said. "Then no matter what happens, we will always get up together in the morning. We'll always be by each other's side."

"I promise," I said tenderly. Hector lay down behind me and wrapped his arms around me.

"You're my best friend, Shell. I love you," he whispered into my ear.

"You're my best friend too," I said. We fell asleep in that position, holding each other.

The next day, we were out to lunch with my sister Laura, and Macho couldn't stop talking about wanting to do another reality TV show.

"Listen, Macho, if you really want a reality show, you have to do something that is like other hits. Think of *Flava Flav*. I watch that show all the time. You can call it *Macho Time*! Just promise me you won't fall in love with someone else," I said, not liking the idea of Hector being filmed all day and surrounded by new people.

"Yeah, like you would ever let that happen," Hector said with a laugh and a twinkle in his eye.

"I'm serious, Macho. I know how long you've been trying. Think of *Macho Time*! I think it could work."

The next Friday, he went to Mexicantown himself to pick up his cocaine. We went out to dinner at Benihana and then came home. We spent that night just lying around. It was too hot to do much else, and he was leaving in the morning. I didn't want him to go.

We lay there for a minute to catch our breaths, but we didn't want to sleep. I stayed up for as long as I could and then drifted off. When I woke up, he was lying next to me, and there was Popsicle juice all over the sheets.

I drove Hector to the airport that morning. He made me promise that I would join him soon. I so desperately didn't want him to leave. As soon as he got on the plane, I went to my son's apartment. I reiterated to my boys that as soon as I got them a house, I was moving to Puerto Rico with Macho.

"Go now," my eldest son said, approving of the idea.

"I need to get you a small house before I go," I replied, surprised that he would say it.

The boys understood why I hesitated, but I was still conflicted. I went home and cried for two days. I missed Hector so much.

A month later, I got a call from Macho. It turned out that they loved the reality show idea. He told me to check YouTube. They already did a trailer for *It's Macho Time*. There was one quote in particular when I was watching the trailer that nearly destroyed me.

"I have everything that I always wanted in life," he said. "But I don't think I've ever really been in love."

I thought I'd be sick. I went absolutely crazy. I called Macho on the phone, then I called his apartment in Puerto Rico. I left him a stern message.

"Fuck you, Macho! Fuck you, fuck you, fuck you, fuck you!" There were some other expletives that I threw in that I can't even remember. Macho called me back immediately. He was laughing.

"Mama, the producers told me to say that! Relax." I hung up the phone on him. I didn't want to hear it.

At some point, I was inclined to believe him, and the talking and phone sex continued. I would send him pictures of me naked. This was the only contact that we had because we were both so busy.

# CHAPTER 9

In December, Macho said that he needed to see me, so he called me every day till I caved in. I was still working seven days a week, ten to twelve hours a day. I had stopped working at the bar. I figured that what I made in overtime compensated for the bar job.

I flew down to Puerto Rico finally, but before I left, I went and picked up a beautiful rosary for Hector's mom and a sterling silver cross necklace for Macho.

He picked me up at the airport in his red jeep with flames on the side. He was waiting at the gate for me. As soon as I got off, my heart dropped to my knees. Every time we met like that, it was as though I hadn't seen him in years. We picked up my luggage and headed to his mama's house in Bayamon. I told him I'd rather stay at the condo in Isla Verde, but Hector refused. He said it was because his mom was there.

The moment we opened the sliding glass doors to the living room, we undressed. I left my tank top on because I didn't want his mom to see me naked. Macho didn't care though. He had opened a bottle of wine for me while he did cocaine. We lay on the futon with my feet toward his head, his head toward my feet. We talked the night away.

When his mom finally got up, we switched to the bedroom, and she took the futon. She insisted.

The following night, we went out to dinner at a restaurant near the condo. We did this a couple of times and always took his mom with us.

One day Macho took me down to the taxi stand because he had a friend there who drove him around town. We made arrangements to go out that night.

Macho, his friend, and I went to this little club in downtown Puerto Rico. It was very scary. The club was off the beaten path, and I was not too happy to be there. We got in a fight because I wanted to go home, and Hector was having too much fun playing pool.

"If we can win this game, then we can go home," Hector said to me, and then he made me play too. I cleared the table in three turns, and we got to leave.

The next day, I went down to the beach, had lunch and a few beers at an open bar, and just enjoyed the serenity of it all. While I was there, this gentleman tried to pick me up.

"I'm here with my fiancé," I said. "I'm not interested."

Now this guy was very persistent, so I finally had to leave and walk away. He followed me down to the beach, so I made a beeline back to my room. When I told Macho what happened, he went down to the beach with me the next day. We stopped for lunch at the very same place. He was looking for the guy who never showed up.

One night Macho was in the living room with his mom, and I was reading in the bedroom.

"It turns me on to watch you read," he said to me. He loved it.

I was trying to lure him into the bedroom for sex, but I didn't want his mom to know, so I kept sending him sexy pictures of me in the mirror. Little did I know that the phone was not on, so I finally had to go to the living room in my sexy thigh highs, heels, bra, and panties. I crept around the door, and Hector was sitting with his mom. He caught a glimpse of me, and I ran back into the room.

"I want to go out," he said. I sighed. All that effort for nothing. But I dressed and left in the jeep. It was funny, the things I used to do in those days to get his attention.

Hector drove to this run-down side of town with small huts and trailers. He told me that he would be back in two minutes and to keep my eyes open. I was absolutely terrified. As soon as he was back in the jeep, my heart was pounding.

"Is this where you got shot at last time?" I asked.

"Yes," he replied. This was the start of an argument.

"You can take chances with your own life, but when I am with you, you cannot take me there!" I said, on the verge of tears. "I do not want to be in the wrong place at the wrong time."

Hector just started laughing. "You're with me, mama," he said. "Nothing is going to happen. I am the Macho Man, and they love me here."

"Not here. Not in this place, Macho. It's evil here. Take me back to the condo."

Hector complied, but first, he made a little pit stop. Of course he did. It was this place that looked like garages or something, but I think that they were actually bars. We pulled up in the driveway and went in and had a beer.

The whole time, I was thinking, *Please just let me get back safe to the condo. Just get me out of here.*

After one beer, we left. Hector and I fought the whole way home. This was the same driveway he later got shot in.

"How dare you put my life in jeopardy!" I yelled. "My children already lost their father, and I can't take any chances with my life." Hector did the usual thing—he laughed at me.

"You are crazy," he said.

The next day, I went down to the beach again. It had become a refuge. I walked down to the restaurant and bought Hector and his mom something to eat for later. Macho finally got out of bed, and we walked hand in hand down the street, looking for ice cream.

We bought some wine at CVS. Since it was my last night, I didn't want to go out. I just wanted to stay in and enjoy my man. His mom understood this because she went to the house and left the condo to us.

Hector and I went downstairs and took a shower, then we went upstairs and got undressed. The sliding glass door remained open, and we turned on the music and lit some candles. Together, we just ate and drank wine, he did his cocaine, and we discussed the book.

He wanted to know again when I was going to move to Puerto Rico permanently.

"I have a job now, mama. I can take care of you," he said to me. At the time, he was still working for *El Gordo y la Flaca*.

"The only missing thing is you," Macho told me. "I hate it when it's time for you to leave, because I never know when I am going to see you again."

"Just give me a little more time, Macho," I said.

We hardly slept. The next morning, we went to try and find Leandry. We went down to the building that he owned, but yet again, he wasn't there. When we were pulling out, the police pulled us over.

My heart started pounding. It turned out that Macho had improper plates on his jeep, so we had to park it and walk back to the hotel. I was furious. I was afraid that I would miss my flight, and there were no cabs around. We kept walking till we could finally hail a cab, and we went back to the condo to get my luggage. He kissed me goodbye, and I just barely made my flight.

Although I was happy that the timing worked out, I was really sad when I got home. I went to visit my kids and told them that in six months' time, I was going to live with Macho in Puerto Rico, at Isla Verde. The very thought of it filled me with happiness, a new beginning, hope.

I returned to my intense work schedule and then took Sundays off to go to church and do volunteer work. These things were new to me, but they just filled my soul in a way.

Macho was doing so great. He was filming his reality show and was a big hit on *El Gordo y la Flaca*. Phone calls and phone sex and sexy pictures continued. But we longed to be together.

Macho finally flew to Detroit in July. There wasn't much time, and he was till so upset by what happened between him and his ex and his kids. I'm not sure which hurt him more in the end, the ex or the kids.

It wasn't long before I had enough money to put a down payment on a house. My realtor was wonderful and found a three-bedroom brick house close to my kids. Finally, I could move to Puerto

Rico, find a job, and make payments from abroad. Everything was falling into place. I called Macho in November.

"I am so glad you called, Shell," he said to me. "I am so depressed. I am sitting here, and I can't get hard."

I knew that Macho was depressed for several reasons, but I guess the inability to be aroused was one of them.

"I sent some girl to get me food, and she started crying, saying, 'I ain't got no money!' That broke bitch."

"Macho, that's not nice," I replied.

"Come on, mama. Make me come," he said childishly. He was having a tantrum. "I need to sleep. Put me to sleep, Shell."

We had phone sex, and Hector had the happy ending that he was looking for. Once he was finally calmed, he was talking sensibly.

"It's time, mama," he said. "I need to see you make your reservation and come see your man."

"I will, Macho."

"I am serious, Shell. I need you. I need to see you. It's time."

"I promise to look for tickets soon," I said. It felt good to be so needed by Macho, and I knew that we'd be together soon.

I called again on Tuesday morning, and that girl answered the phone. I asked if Macho was there, and she hung up immediately. I let it go. It was something I could no longer control. And I told myself that when we live together, it would be different. Everything would change.

That was the funny thing about me and Macho. We were always going in opposite directions, just waiting to come together.

It was a Tuesday night. I'll never forget it. I was hanging out at the bar where my sister worked, playing pool and drinking. My sister Ila called, and there was something strange in her voice.

"Have you heard, Shell?" she said.

"Heard what?" I replied. I was instantly uneasy.

"Turn on the news," Ila said. It sounded like she was on the verge of tears. "I'm so sorry, Shell."

"What the hell are you talking about?" I said, desperately wanting to know what was going on.

"Macho's been shot."

I didn't hear her right. Did she fumble with her words? Or was I just not able to make sense of it?

I ran outside, into the fresh air, and asked her to repeat herself.

"Macho's been shot in the head," she said.

Time stood still. I felt my knees giving way, and things were spinning, but I ran inside the bar to turn on the TV.

There it was. Macho was all over the news. I just sat there and stared blankly. At first, I was in shock, but once the tears came, they rained down uncontrollably. My friend Al held me in his arms for what felt like an eternity.

I called my sister Dana immediately and demanded that she get me a flight to Puerto Rico. She tried her best, but it was Thanksgiving, and there were no seats. I called Linda's and Angie's phones to see what the hell was going on.

Angie's assistant spoke with me, and she said that Hector was in surgery and that she'd call me back. I was frantic, alone, and afraid that I might lose my mind. I sat by the phone, waiting for it to ring. Friends bought be shots and sat next to me. I threw the shots back, desperate to be numb, desperate to calm down. Finally, I just wanted to go home, so they drove me back.

I searched the computer, frantically looking for information. At one point, the sheer exhaustion made me drift off into sleep.

Macho came to me that night, in my dream. He held me in his arms.

"I have to go, mama," he said tenderly.

"I don't want you to leave," I said to him, and Macho gave me that amazing smile.

When I woke up, it was like I was being jerked painfully back into my body, back into reality. I ran to my computer and searched desperately for new information. My sister finally called.

"He went into cardiac arrest," she said. "He is strong, so you don't have to worry."

I knew in that moment that he was gone. The realization came over me quite quickly. The reason that I knew? Macho had abused his body so badly over the years that he wasn't going to pull through. He took too many punches, both outside and inside.

I believe that Macho came to me in my dream in order to say goodbye. I'm grateful that he did that, but it wouldn't protect me from the pain. There would be no Puerto Rico, no marriage, no future together.

I got a call from Angie's assistant. "I don't want you to hear this on the news. Macho is in bad shape, and they don't think he is going to make it." She didn't have to say it. I already knew.

I said goodbye to my baby that night and he said goodbye to me before anyone else could say goodbye.

It felt like the tears would never stop falling. I went to my sister's for Thanksgiving just to have an excuse to stop crying and to be around other people, since I was too afraid to be alone.

Now keep in mind, everyone was still holding out hope, even though I was sure. I remember baking pies for Thanksgiving just to be in the world of the living. There's something soothing about baking. Everyone was so warm and gracious, telling me to keep praying and thinking good thoughts. But my mind was elsewhere. I even forgot to cook the pumpkin pie I prepared.

When the news finally came out that Hector had passed, it would have been nice to just grieve in peace, but there was nothing peaceful about Macho's family. There were so many women in the family that fought over him.

I called Betsy, his sister-in-law, and she told me that his body was being brought to New York. I called Jazzy, his niece, and she connected me with Macho's sister.

"I'm coming to New York," I said. I wouldn't miss it for the world. I wanted to speak with his mother, Maria, but I knew that she must be too out of it. I could only imagine how that blow landed on her.

It was hard watching all those girls fight over him. People assumed Macho would have enjoyed it, but I know better. He wanted to escape from all that. He was trying to create a new life and image for himself. He just ran out of time.

# EPILOGUE

I was still in a fog when we touched down in LaGuardia, stayed at an airport hotel that night, and took a cab to the funeral home the next morning. The media had already gathered outside when I arrived.

"Who are you?" one photographer said.

"I'm his woman," I said fearlessly as I got out of the cab. The guy probably thought I was rash or crazy, but Hector would have been so proud of me. I turned and walked into the funeral home, dodging cameras.

No one was there yet, and Macho was not ready for viewing. It was surreal being there alone. I had no sense of time or place. They let me come in and wait so I wouldn't have to deal with more reporters.

After some time, I was standing outside when Hector Jr. and Macho's mother came up the stairs. I hugged Hector Jr. and started crying. Maria grabbed me.

"I waited for you to come to Puerto Rico," Hector's mother said through her tears.

"There were no flights. I had to wait to come to New York," I said, hoping that this explanation would be enough. Maria became hysterical.

"They took him, Shelly. They took my baby," she cried, falling into my arms.

"I know. They took my baby too," I said. We held each other desperately, wishing that it was all some kind of bad dream.

Hector Jr. took me aside. "You belong here, Shelly," he said tenderly. "My father would want you here, and if anybody messes with you, you are with me," Junior said. Of course, I knew I had every right to be there, but Hector Jr. was smart. He knew what I was up against. Amy would give me a hard time.

Once we were all inside, Macho's best friend George held me till I stopped crying. Everyone was there, and Hector was ready for viewing. I didn't know how I'd be able to do it. Rudy, Hector's bodyguard, was a big guy and strong enough to hold me as I walked up to the casket when I was ready. I carried an all-white rosary.

"May I leave it in the casket with Macho?" I asked Maria.

"Of course," she said, squeezing my hand.

I waited till everyone was done, then I stepped forward, Rudy holding me tight. I looked down at him and did my best to stay strong. I put the rosary in his hands, now cold. Those hands had fought so hard in this world, and now they could rest. I kissed them. They had been so much a part of my life. Then I kissed his lips and his forehead, and in my heart, not aloud, I said goodbye.

As I said, there had been so many arrivals and departures, separations and reunions between Macho and I. That was the last goodbye.

With the private viewing done, it was time to face the public. There were thousands of people on the sidewalks.

Macho's casket was draped in the Puerto Rican flag, and his two youngest sons also waved the same flag as we paraded through East Harlem. His body was carried in a white horse-drawn carriage.

The love of his fans was overwhelming and so beautiful to see. Macho would have been proud. Fans outside the church were chanting and waiting to say goodbye to their hero. Sammy came in, and when I saw him, I broke down again.

Jerry Villarreal and Jerry Jr. finally got there in the evening. Bless Junior. He flew a red-eye from Vegas and then drove from Detroit with his father. We were sitting in the front row, just like I used to do at Macho's fights. It was Sammy, Leo, Jerry Sr., Jerry Jr., and a childhood friend named PeeWee. I was called aside before the service began and told that they didn't have the money to bury Macho. I couldn't believe what I was hearing.

Linda was trying to get emergency money out of his account but wasn't able to. I sat back down and told both Jerrys what was happening. That was when PeeWee said that he wanted to pay for it. I was so filled with gratitude in that moment that I didn't have the words.

At the cemetery, there was someone I never wanted to see: Bonita Money. My first instinct was to go make her leave, but Macho's sisters knocked some sense into me. We'd fight with our heads, not our hands. She was never served for her crime because Macho didn't have her address. I sent Macho's friend Panchito over there to tell her some fluff so that he could get the address out of her and her phone number.

From a distance, I just looked at her and smiled. Macho always wanted to get back at her, and little did he know that it wouldn't be till his funeral.

We waited forever for PeeWee to come back with the money. In fact, the whole procession was waiting.

Once he had it, I went into the office where he was settling the bill and just gave him the biggest hug. It was the most beautiful thing any human being could do.

However heartening the cameras and fans were, it was overwhelming. There were questions about book deals and other things like that, but it was not the time or place for such talk. Of course, Macho himself would have jumped on the opportunity! But he wasn't going to get his way on that day.

I waited till the people and cameras were gone, and then Sammy, Reggie, Leo, and I went up to Macho's casket. I was holding a flower that Sammy gave me, and when everyone was gone, I got down on my knees and laid the flower on the coffin.

"Please take care of my baby," I said, looking up to the heavens. I wanted Macho to rest with the Lord. He wasn't perfect in this life, but he was my angel. I looked down at Macho. "I will see you in heaven," I said, already looking forward to the day.

Being at the airport, ready to go home to Detroit, felt oddly right. Airports were my favorite place to meet Macho after a long time apart. I went to a bar and ordered some Patrón. I raised the glass to Hector.

But the flight home was like torture. The reality was hitting hard. I was so upset when I got home that I couldn't find my car at the airport. My son had to come and get me to find it. It was right where I had left it in the front row, but it was like I couldn't see straight. When I got home, I stayed in bed for three days. I tried to go to work, I tried to eat and sleep, but I couldn't. It was like my heart was missing.

You know, people told me a lot that they were sorry for me. But I wasn't sorry. I was happy for the pain that I felt, because that pain told me how much I loved and how blessed I was that I was able to love someone with all my heart.

It took a major car accident to force me to get the rest I needed and to reminisce about things. There was that manuscript that Macho and I were working on. I couldn't stop thinking about it. Was I strong enough to go through it? Would I be able to tell it clearly? It seemed overwhelming, but maybe it was a chance to relive it all one more time. And deep down, I needed to, for myself, to move forward.

Macho passed in November, and in January I got hit by a drunk driver. I was out of work for three months. The first week, I lay in bed crying. The second week, I woke up in bed, and in my head, I thanked God for giving me this time to write the book. I realized how everything happens for a reason. God was giving me time to finally finish the book.

I put the poster boards back up on the wall in my new office. I was in so much pain from the accident and losing the love of my life that I would go to the liquor store and buy a fifth of vodka. I would stay up for days drinking and crying and writing, then I would sleep for a few days. This went on for two weeks, and then I finished. I did it. I finally wrote the book.

I have to admit that in writing this, I have laughed out loud, I have cried my eyes out, I have hated Macho so much, and I've fallen in love with him all over again. Our story was not smooth or clean. It was rocky, tempestuous, and fully alive. What we shared was as crazy and amazing as life itself. We didn't pull any punches.

I was so lucky to have him in my life. I got to live a life I would have never dreamed of. I actually realize how lucky I was that it hurt so bad. That meant that I loved so much. Some people will never in their life feel love like that.

After my accident, people started telling me that I have the worst luck. I had to laugh. Without the injury, I would never have written these memories. Collisions happen for a reason. Things break open so that they can come back together. I see that now.

It makes me think of the night when I was weak and tired and felt impulsive enough to drive with friends to a casino to watch a fight. That was where I met Hector Camacho. I was lost, and Macho found me. I became his woman, and he became my man.

Some things are forever.

# LADY AND THE TEN-TIME WORLD CHAMP

# LADY AND THE TEN-TIME WORLD CHAMP

## LADY AND THE TEN-TIME WORLD CHAMP

## LADY AND THE TEN-TIME WORLD CHAMP

## LADY AND THE TEN-TIME WORLD CHAMP

# SHELLY SALEMASSI

## LADY AND THE TEN-TIME WORLD CHAMP

## LADY AND THE TEN-TIME WORLD CHAMP

# LADY AND THE TEN-TIME WORLD CHAMP

## LADY AND THE TEN-TIME WORLD CHAMP

## LADY AND THE TEN-TIME WORLD CHAMP

## LADY AND THE TEN-TIME WORLD CHAMP

## SHELLY SALEMASSI

## LADY AND THE TEN-TIME WORLD CHAMP

# SHELLY SALEMASSI

# LADY AND THE TEN-TIME WORLD CHAMP

## LADY AND THE TEN-TIME WORLD CHAMP

## LADY AND THE TEN-TIME WORLD CHAMP

# LADY AND THE TEN-TIME WORLD CHAMP

## LADY AND THE TEN-TIME WORLD CHAMP

# LADY AND THE TEN-TIME WORLD CHAMP

# ABOUT THE AUTHOR

Shelly Salemassi was in a personal relationship with the famous boxer Hector "Macho" Camacho for fifteen years. She was engaged to him in 2012 when he was shot in a drive-by shooting in Bayamon, Puerto Rico. She currently resides in Detroit, Michigan, where she works as a senior title closer for Titleocity. She has worked in the real estate industry for over twenty-five years. She is a licensed notary and holds a resident producer license for the state of Michigan.

CPSIA information can be obtained
at www.ICGtesting.com
Printed in the USA
LVHW090007100222
710541LV00022B/89